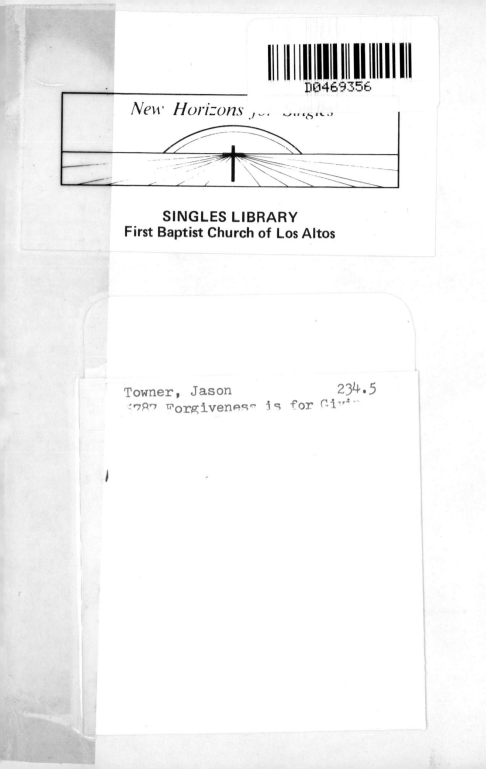

New Horizons for Singles

SINGLES LIBRARY
First Baptist Church of Los Altos

FORGIVENESS
Is For
GIVING

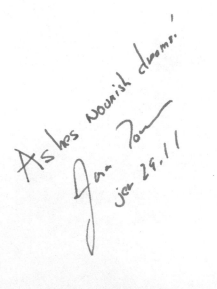

Ashes nourish dreams!
Dana Torr
jan 29, 11

Other books by the author:

Warm Reflections
A Part of Me Is Missing
Jason Loves Jane (But They Got A Divorce)
One-Parent Families

FORGIVENESS
IS FOR
GIVING

Jason Towner

**impact
books**

Nashville, TN

First printing April 1982

Bible verses marked NIV are from the HOLY BIBLE, *New International Version*,
copyright © 1978, New York Bible Society. Used by permission.

Verses marked (LB) are from *The Living Bible*, copyright © 1971, Tyndale House
Publishers, Wheaton, Illinois. Used by permission.

Quotation from Sidney Jourard is taken from *The Transparent Self* published by
Van Nostrand Reinhold Co., p. 5.

14027p

Library of Congress Cataloging in Publication Data
Towner, Jason.
    Forgiveness is for giving.

    1. Forgiveness. I. Title.
BJ1476.T68   234'.5   81-84923
ISBN 0-914850-56-3   AACR2

Cover Design by Maribeth Wright
Interior Design by Nancye Willis

Distributed by The Zondervan Corporation

This book is dedicated
to all the pilgrims
I have met
on the road
to forgiveness
—not as an abstract ideal
but as a reality!

Contents

Foreword

By his own admission Jason Towner calls himself a novice in the art of forgiveness. In fact, with genuine humility, he says: "Please do not call me an expert. If you do, I will only disappoint you . . ."

However, in this touching, sensitive, and highly perceptive book, Jason Towner's expertise on forgiveness is as beautiful as it is rare.

Only a person whose heart has been minced into bits and pieces and then been thoroughly healed and restored by God could take the overpreached and overworked concepts of forgiveness and make them sparkle with delicious freshness.

Listen to this handful of statements:

Forgiveness is always a decision.
Forgiveness is as natural as the softness of a baby's skin.
It's unforgiveness that is a learned behavior.
Unforgiveness is suicidal (and still a decision).
Forgiveness is a journey—not a destination.

Oh, dear Jason, there are so many of us who need to bathe in what you call "the healing waters in the fountain of forgiveness." It is there, in the cleansing of those waters, that we are enabled by God to get on with our lives as His children.

Thank you for your seminars and for this book! We have much to learn from you.

—JOYCE LANDORF

Preface

You are my brother/my sister.
Are you the one who so desperately needs
    to find a way to say "Forgive me,"
    but is torn by a feeling in the pit of the stomach
    that time is running out. . . ?
Or are you the one who needs to *forgive,*
    and, with your defenses up, insist,
    "But you don't understand!"
    "If it had happened to you . . ."?
If so, you are like a prisoner in solitary confinement,
    caged in your damp, dark tomb,
    coveting a pindrop of light.
You wait there in your quiet hell,
    wondering if relief will ever come . . .
Your silent sighs are my invitation
    to model forgiveness.
To remember the One who once stepped into
    the darkness of *my* cell,
    turned on the light,
    and, without condemnation, went to work!
Because I know the Forgiver, I have found the way . . .

Be gentle and ready to forgive; never hold grudges. Remember, the Lord forgave you, so you must forgive others.

(Col. 3:13 LB)

Special Thanks

I owe a debt of thanks to those who typed drafts of this manuscript: Lori Tupper, Beth Scott, Carol Ward, and Elspeth Ayrd.

A special word of thanks to Dr. Paul Bassett, professor of church history at Nazarene Theological Seminary, who has a unique way of unlocking great biblical truths.

And a special thanks to those who have openly challenged or confronted me—for they helped me clarify my thoughts and convinced me of the need for someone to say, "Forgiveness Is For Giving."

Finally, kind words for two sensitive editors— Ann Severance and Nancye Willis—who gave countless hours to discussing these concepts and to editing the manuscript.

And to a lady named Jane who helped me forgive myself.

I

Forgiveness:
The Promise
and the Principles

The Promise of Forgiveness

You can be forgiven!
"Not for what I've done . . ."
"No one knows except . . ."
"I don't even want to think about it!"
You can forgive!
"Never!"
"But you don't understand!"
"After what he did . . ."
Forgiveness is a decision.

Who suffers more—those who can't *forgive* or those who can't *accept forgiveness?* The word *can't*—although a contraction—is a contradiction, a decision. "I can't forgive you . . ." is the ultimate ego trip which declares: "What has happened to me makes me really important. I'm a martyr!" Martyrdom is fertilizer for revenge.

Refusing to give or accept

forgiveness is foolish, shortsighted, and most of all, selfish. God's greatest gift is forgiveness. Forgiveness has always been on God's agenda.

If you read the Word, it's all there: Every act possible—rape, murder, homosexuality, incest, betrayal, lust, perversion, embezzlement—is recorded at the direction of the Holy Spirit.

It's all recorded in the Word for one reason: To let us know that there is no human experience that is not common to mankind, or which can elude the healing and hope of the Lord.

The Word is the Lifebook, the Sourcebook, filled with stories of people just like you and me, minus permanent-press shirts, cologne, deodorant, cars. But we do have some things in common with the biblical characters:

- Those moments of ultimate solitude just before we sleep
- The searching for identity
- The longing for intimacy, for closeness to another
- Fear and guilt—"What if someone finds out about . . .?"

The Lord knows that our insecurities may cause us to dwell upon a "wounding," and because of it, become spiritual hermits. Precisely because He loves us, He confronts us and *"devises ways* so that a banished person may not remain estranged from him" (2 Sam. 14:14 NIV, *italics mine*). He longs for our wholeness. He wants us to live abundantly and redemptively and has proven it through at least four supreme acts:

1. He allowed Adam and Eve to live after their disobedience.

Have you ever wondered why God didn't just bring down fire from heaven and destroy Adam and Eve and their garden home?

Why didn't God just throw them out
    as we would rotten apples?
Who would have known?
Why didn't He start all over again
    with a new Adam and a new Eve?
Perhaps because of the eternal truth:
    "God is love, God is love . . ."
God would have known.

And there was some strange affinity
    between God and His creation: Man and
    woman.
It was the promise of forgiveness.

Forgiveness had never before existed
    until the moment of failure and sin.

And whatever else historians have written
    about the day Adam and Eve
    were driven from the garden,
There was another side:
    Forgiveness was born in the twilight of that
    day.

2. He allowed the world to crucify His Son.
The supreme example of God's forgiveness came
on that first Good Friday as His Son hung suspended
between the worlds. The laughter of hell invaded
heaven during Jesus' hours of suffering on the cross. In
that moment Satan yelled across the chasm:
    "Now what are You going to do?"
    God could have responded with a divine scream:
"No! You cannot do this to My Son and get away with
it!"
    Just His thought could have destroyed those who
had mocked the Son and had driven the spikes through
His hands.
    For a brief moment, Satan thought he had won

the contest. He believed he had goaded God to the point of intervening, aborting the plan, canceling His Son's love message to the world. Satan really thought he had won—his thirty-three years of scheming to sabotage or negate Jesus' ministry had finally paid off.

In that moment, God looked down through the hallways of history and He saw—you. He saw your need of a Savior and He didn't want one more person to struggle under the futility of the law, suffering the tyranny of "an eye for an eye, a tooth for a tooth."

All the inhabitants of hell stood on tiptoe for a better look. Silence.

Then God turned away.

3. The Father allowed His Son to die.

The smile froze on Satan's lips; he knew he had lost. His days of power were numbered.

Jesus marched through hell in an expedition of love, piercing its darkness with a glimmer of hope. The condemned realized that their descendants could now avoid their place of torment through this One.

4. The Father allows us to receive or reject His forgiveness!

What would it mean, what could it really mean, if you could know *this moment,* you were forgiven? What would it mean this moment if you could release that grudge, that burden you have carried for so long?

Because God decided to allow these things to happen, we are forever linked to forgiveness. *If anyone ever had the right to declare:*

- "This takes the cake . . ."
- "After all I've done for you . . ."
- "This is the last straw . . ."
- "You can't do this and get away with it . . ."

God had that right. But He chose not to claim it.

That Good Friday God saw all of us who struggle with forgiveness in our own lives.

"You just don't understand," we often say to people who reject our claims to martyrdom. "If it had happened to you," we suggest, "then you'd think differently." Many have had a lot of practice. Some can use such harshness, such venom, that the words steam before they sting.

"What if it had been *your* daughter who was raped?"

"What if it had been *your* son who was killed?"

"What if it had been *your* wife who ran away with another man?"

Well?

Some people plead their application for martyrdom in such a way that we feel guilty denying their request.

But God listens to all our noise—our yelling and screaming and cursing—because He's been there. *He does understand,* even though, perhaps when the griping and complaining of the world get too loud, He "changes channels" and tunes in to hear the giggles of a young child charging the waves or wrestling with a litter of puppies.

That Good Friday, maybe God saw Jason Towner—a kid who would grow up scarred by an unforgiving spirit.

I grew up in the pre-Spock era. My parents never read books on child psychology, relying instead on the prevailing theory of child-rearing, simple and easily memorized: "Spare the rod, spoil the child."

The baby of the family, with a sister twelve years older and a brother four years older than I, I had a good thing going.

Then my sister eloped and later had a son. The young family moved in with us. My parents gave up their bedroom and my brother and I "graciously consented" to give our bedroom to my parents. I resented that move to a folding bed in the corner of the dining room as much as I resented the aggressiveness of this new little guy who had invaded our world.

One morning my sister put my nephew in bed with me, and for some reason, I hit him. My dad, who thought his first grandson was pretty special, couldn't believe his eyes! Unfortunately for me, I tried to further his disbelief by denying that I had hit the baby—quite a mistake in logic!

In the next few moments I came to experientially understand (bottom first; head later) that my dad loved his grandson as much as he loved his son. When I refused dad's invitation to say, "I'm sorry" (from my perspective, it made little sense to apologize to a four-month-old baby), he lifted me up and out of that rollaway and I felt a part of me "strangely warmed." My dad lit into me like a chainsaw on a fallen log destined for firewood.

And that whipping hurt more than my physical being—it also stung my soul deep *within me,* leaving wounds resistant to healing.

That Good Friday, God saw those who would experience unmentionable and, therefore, unforgiven sins and hurts.

Forever condemning themselves, forever mentally replaying those sins and hurts after an evangelist or pastor's solemn declaration following a fruitless seven-verse invitation: "I have the feeling there is someone here who . . .", they can *never* forget.

God saw the weak,
     the frail,
     the naïve,
     the lonely,
     the oppressed.

God saw all the psychologically whipped of the future and realized they needed Someone to wipe away their tears, to cleanse their sins, to heal their memories.

Somehow God saw all of us who would live unlike the King's kids He designed us to be.

And He realized only one Person could restore our full heirship—His Son.

His Son died . . . and heaven was silent.

God has never regretted that decision.

If anyone ever had a right to hold a grudge, God did. He had sent His only Son on a thirty-three-year mission into the world—to die.

Why hadn't Jesus been killed in the manger by a sword of cruel Herod? Wouldn't the blood of the Baby Jesus have saved us as readily as that of an adult Jesus?

He died as an adult so that He could understand us, as well as redeem us. *And to help us understand that He understands.*

God had every right to a grudge. His Son had healed the sick, the lame, the deaf, the blind. His Son had fed, spiritually and physically, the multitudes and the world. And, to show its gratitude, the multitudes and the world executed Him.

So, if God forgave and continues to forgive—what is it that you can't forgive?

What stops you?

What event, what experience, what attitude has bound you with transparent chains?

Forgiveness is not an abstract ideal, but a reality. Forgiveness is always a decision.

You can forgive!
You can be forgiven!
You can receive!
You can give!

The Principles of
Forgiveness

I believe that our theology shapes our understanding of forgiveness. A theology or psychology of forgiveness is forever linked to the God who is rooted in forgiving, whose very nature is forgiveness.

Some ministers preach from an agenda, knowing first what they want to say and then finding Scripture that supports their thoughts, directly or indirectly.

When I was a child, our minister often emptied his arsenal on the subject of women's clothing—what they wore (and didn't wear) and how they wore it. One favorite passage related the story of David and Bathsheba. From his perspective, it was all the woman's fault. "What could she expect, taking a bath right out in the back yard?" he demanded.

That childhood minister read 2 Samuel 11 with an agenda— a set of preconceived notions—

so that it portrayed not a God of forgiveness but a God of wrath. As a result of this method, God is seen leaning over the portals of glory waiting to take a swing at us.

Years later, for different reasons, that passage has become my favorite. For me, 2 Samuel is one of the greatest expositions of God as forgiver. Thus the Creator, the God of Genesis, is revealed as a God deeply concerned about our personal struggles.

PRINCIPLE 1: *Responsibility precedes forgiveness.*

The chapter opens, clearly assigning responsibility to David. "In the spring, at the time when kings go off to war" (2 Sam. 11:1 NIV), David remained home. *If* David had been in the fields with his troops rather than at the palace, the entire episode would not have taken place. But for some reason, he "tarried" in Jerusalem, waiting for the time he would be ready to assume field command of the battle against the enemies of Israel.

If anyone had quizzed him at that particular point about how things were going spiritually, David would have denied any serious concern. "I'm just not ready for this war. In a few days, I'll read some positive-thinking books, and go down and fight." Besides little was accomplished in the first days anyway. The suggestion that his lack of preparedness could bring grave consequences would have caused him to laugh.

One sleepless night, from his vantage point on the roof of the palace, David observed a beautiful woman bathing. It was not wrong to recognize her beauty— after all, he *was* a man. However, the *second lingering* look aroused his passions. He made a decision to prolong his insomnia and sent someone to find out about her.

That informer reported, "Isn't this Bathsheba, the daughter of Eliam and the wife of Uriah the Hittite?" (2 Sam. 11:3 NIV). The fact that she was someone's daughter and, more importantly, someone's wife (and the mention of specific names suggests their recognition by David) *should* have short-circuited his passion.

But he rejected the "stop signs" or "caution" warnings and called for her. As king, he slept with her *even* as her husband defended his kingdom on the field of battle. In David's thinking, all of the kingdom was his.

David refused to shoulder the blame fully. (She shouldn't have been out there in the first place!) "Against you, you only, have I sinned" (Ps. 51:4 NIV) was his desperate prayer. But he was also guilty of sinning against Bathsheba *and* Uriah.

Bathsheba's resulting pregnancy caused David, perhaps in panic, to carry his deceit a step further.

Rather than admit his sins (plural—lust, adultery), he spun a cover-up. He sent for Uriah, requested an account of the battle, and then sent the warrior home to Bathsheba. Perhaps the king grinned as he congratulated himself on the simplicity of his plan. "Nine months from now, who'll know the difference?" he might have reasoned.

Uriah, however, did not go inside his palace, but slept with the servants at the entrance. The next morning David confronted him, saying: "Haven't you just come from a distance? Why didn't you go home?" (2 Sam. 11:10 NIV).

Maybe Uriah thought that David was testing his character. Maybe he thought proudly: *Others might enjoy the comforts of home, but my character and devotion to duty are impeccable!* And then he voiced his thoughts:

> "The ark and Israel and Judah are staying in tents, and my master Joab and my lord's men are camped in

open fields. How could I go to my house and eat and drink and lie with my wife. As surely as you live, I will not do such a thing!"   (2 Sam. 11:11 NIV)

In David's day, abstinence was believed to give soldiers physical strength as well as the added incentive to end the battle in order to return to their homes.

So David escalated his plot by having Uriah stay over another day, to dine with him at the palace. David gave him wine, reasoning that an intoxicated Uriah wouldn't be able to remember what had happened. In nine months, how could Uriah deny fatherhood of Bathsheba's child?

Yet even drunk, Uriah kept the soldier's code, sleeping "on his mat among his master's servants; he did not go home" (2 Sam. 11:13 NIV).

In a moment of desperation, David drafted a letter that became Uriah's death warrant. He ordered Joab to put Uriah in a dangerous position with the enemy and then to withdraw supporting troops. Uriah returned to Joab, obviously unaware of the plot.

Thus what began as an act of unpreparedness
        became lust
        became adultery
        became conspiracy
        became murder, premeditated.
(And men continue to think they can "control" or limit sin and its consequences!)

How anxiously David must have awaited word of the implementation of his order! Finally a messenger arrived to report, "The men overpowered us . . . some of the king's men died. Moreover, your servant Uriah the Hittite is dead" (2 Sam. 11:23–24 NIV). David sighed in momentary relief. No doubt the messenger also relaxed, having thought the report might anger the king.

When Bathsheba learned of her husband's death, she mourned for him. Then after the appropriate season of mourning and grief, "David *had her* brought to his house, and she became his wife" (2 Sam. 11:27 NIV, *italics mine*).

Did she suspect David's involvement in Uriah's death? Did she consider the death coincidental or convenient? She must have known the penalty for adultery: stoning. But now the plot included hypocrisy. In an era before Social Security or life insurance or welfare, David managed, by taking the grieving widow into his home, to convey the notion that he had acted in gratitude to the brave Uriah, who had given his life in battle for the king.

PRINCIPLE 2: *Forgiveness is confrontational.*

God confronts—that is a basic characteristic of His nature. Although we are not offered psychological insights into David's emotional state, the fear of discovery must have been paralyzing. He must have been miserably relieved with Uriah's death.

The twelfth chapter opens majestically, "The Lord sent Nathan to David" (2 Sam. 12:1 NIV).

(Well, it sounds majestic to those of us who view God's confrontations as positive. During my childhood, my parents occasionally had reasonable evidence that I was guilty of infringement of their rules. Instead of rushing to convene a grand jury, they waited. Often, my misery was so burdensome that I *had* to confess.)

The Word does not give us any hints about the time span of each stage of this story's development. How long did God wait to send Nathan to David?

However long He waits, God's confrontations are always motivated by His love. Our sin breaks God's heart, and because of His godly nature, He must confront us. The psalmist reported, "He does not treat us as our sins deserve or repay us according to our iniquities" (Ps. 103:10 NIV).

Though Uriah's physical body could not return from the dead to confront David, his character could. People began to put two and two together. They realized a man of Uriah's stature, who had publicly refused to go home while on furlough or off in battle, couldn't possibly have a pregnant wife.

In the desert God asked Nathan, a man of integrity, to deliver a message. "Sure, what is it?" he may have replied.

"Go to the palace . . . accuse the king of adultery and murder."

Can you, in your mind's eye, see the surprise on Nathan's face, the color draining? "You want me to confront the king with *that* accusation?" David might not be open to such a blunt message and, after all, Nathan didn't have any real evidence!

However, the Word reports no doubt on the part of Nathan nor the Israelites concerning David's guilt. After all, prophets gained their posts through divine, rather than royal appointment. Perhaps, en route, Nathan began composing his speech. Certainly it took nerves of steel combined with an overwhelming confidence of the Lord's presence to deliver this message.

Many of us carry burdens of unforgiveness because we do not care enough to confront; or we fear being labeled "nosy." Relationships and friendships are sometimes too fragile to risk confrontation.

But confrontation proves that we believe there is still worth in the individual.

PRINCIPLE 3: *Forgiveness is an investment in the potential of the forgiven.*

Why didn't God strike David dead in the act of intercourse with Bathsheba? Probably for the same reason that he doesn't strike you and me dead during our acts of sin and rebellion. God sees our salvageability.

After years of running a salvage business, Martin Mull entered the ministry. He jokingly likened his former profession to his present, saying he had merely exchanged the commodity salvaged. God salvages people and He needs assistants like Martin and Nathan.

Nathan did not confront in stained-glass tones of judgment. Rather, he spoke in a manner designed to appeal to David's background as a shepherd.

> "There were two men in a certain town, one rich and the other poor. The rich had a very large number of sheep and the poor man had nothing except one little ewe lamb he had bought. He raised it, and it grew up with him and his children. It shared his food, drank from his cup and even slept in his arms. It was like a daughter to him.
>
> "Now a traveler came to the rich man, but the rich man refrained from taking one of his own sheep or cattle to prepare a meal for the traveler who had come to him. Instead, he took the ewe lamb that belonged to the poor man and prepared it for the one who had come to him." (2 Sam. 12:1–4 NIV)

The story created an immediate and predictable response within David—an eruption! "As surely as the Lord lives, the man who did this deserves to die! He must pay for the lamb four times over, because he did such a thing and had no pity!" (2 Sam. 12:5–6 NIV).

Nathan breathed a last prayer for strength. Without blinking an eye, he responded, "You are the man!" (2 Sam. 12:7 NIV). Those four words hit David with a tremendous wallop! A king's world crumbled as the prophet described the punishment. How many times had David feared such a moment of nakedness? Had he rehearsed his excuses?

> "Out of your own household, I am going to bring calamity to you.
> "Before your very eyes I will take your wives and give them to one who is close to you, and he will lie with your wives in broad daylight.
> "The son born to you will die."
> (2 Sam. 12:11–14 NIV)

That must have provoked a "Who? What? When? Where?" series of questions. We, too, crave more details. What was David's psychological state? How did Nathan make his exit? Was he not as broken as the king?

So "the Lord struck the child . . ." (2 Sam. 12:15 NIV), an action that must have broken God's heart. David's resulting behavior was predictably characteristic of a grieving father:

(1) David pleaded with God for the child's life.
(2) He fasted.
(3) He spent the nights prostrate on the floor of his home.

PRINCIPLE 4: *Forgiveness is not negotiable.*

We cannot negotiate authentic forgiveness with God or with one another. God has never allowed anyone that privilege, and cannot grant it to you.

David's penitent actions were not those of an immature boy trying to short-circuit the penalties of his sin, but one of an authentic man, "a friend of God," pleading for his child's life. His pleas were as sincere as were those of Abraham when he prepared to sacrifice his son, and supremely demonstrated when God watched His own Son die. God must have wept with David, seeing his anguish as a rehearsal of His own, to be experienced during the three days when His Son lay snugly in death's embrace.

At some point, a foolish king's prayer to save his little child became an equally fervent prayer to save himself. It must have been difficult for the elders of his household to witness David's humiliation; to listen to his confession.

David prayed for seven days, unaware of those around him. Then he noticed "his servants were whispering among themselves and he realized that the child was dead" (2 Sam. 12:19 NIV). The servants reluctantly confirmed the death but were stunned by David's abrupt change in behavior.

> Then David got up from the ground. After he had washed, put on lotions and changed his clothes, he went into the house of the Lord and worshiped. Then he went down to his own house, and at his request, they served him food, and he ate.
>
> (2 Sam. 12:20 NIV)

When questioned by his servants, David answered: "I thought 'Who knows? The Lord may be gracious to me and let the child live'" (2 Sam. 12:22 NIV). David's actions paralleled those of the Israelites in Egypt. "When they heard that the Lord was concerned about them and *had seen their misery*, they bowed down and worshiped" (Exod. 4:31 NIV). The breaking precedes the worship, then *and now*. It is often only in those moments of brokenness that the Lord has our complete attention.

How many have promised, *O God, if You'll get me out of here safely (or if You'll heal me) I'll go to Africa?* But those promises frequently spring from our inventory of fears instead of from God's design for our lives. God may want that person to be His missionary in Cleveland, or some other place less dramatic and exotic than the jungle. Sometimes He prefers the non-grandiose —what we consider the ordinary.

Since we have made a place in our religious folklore for foxhole conversions, realistic forgiveness through God has only one term: unconditional surrender.

PRINCIPLE 5: *Forgiveness is a reality in this world as well as in the next.*

Some people spend their earthly lives waiting for their "pie-in-the-sky-in-the-bye-and-bye." And furthermore, they want it *a la mode!*

But forgiveness is a part of this world as well as the next. It readies us for eternal delights while helping us enjoy this "rehearsal" to eternity's day. The old Southern evangelist Sam Jones suggested that God's forgiveness is like a wagon—it ensures that you will reach your destination while enjoying the ride.

David realized he could not bring the unnamed child back to life, and broke his fast. "I will go to him" (2 Sam. 12:23 NIV), he promised. And we do have the hope that someday we will spend eternity in the company of those with whom we were unable to enjoy this life. Deathbed reconciliations between estranged friends, family, and colleagues are a real tragedy. How easily we forgive as the death stalker approaches!

Then, David comforted Bathsheba: "He went to her and lay with her" (2 Sam. 12:24 NIV). At this point, Bathsheba must have known most, if not all, of the details of David's involvement in Uriah's death.

Perhaps she protested: "Get away from me!" or "Leave me alone!"

Perhaps she was sitting alone in the darkness, softly crying, when David called her name. Can you see David, returning from his confessional prayers, gently speaking her name: "Bathsheba . . . I want to talk to you"?

There *are* difficult moments of confession in a marriage. I recall causing my wife a lot of hurt because of my insensitivity. She had worked long and hard to surprise me with an electric typewriter—a brand-new cartridge model. Instead of showing my gratitude and pleasure, I voiced my concern over the typewriter's cost and the expense of the cartridges. Jane's delight burst like a punctured balloon!

I tried to comfort her, saying over and over, "I'm sorry." Finally I held her as we both cried.

And Bathsheba accepted David's comfort. As a result of the "comforting," Bathsheba eventually gave birth to a son whom they named Solomon.

Two quotations help us see that David and Bathsheba shared forgiveness. "He lay *with* her" (2 Sam. 12:24, *italics mine)* suggests equality of intimacy. "*They* named him Solomon" (2 Sam. 12:24, *italics mine*) reveals equality of response to the child. Generally, in Scripture, one parent named the child.

In the Old Testament, infertility, not pregnancy, was a punishment. Our contemporary views of fertility make it difficult to appreciate the importance placed by these Jews upon God's involvement in conception. Eve explained: *"With the help of the Lord* I have brought forth a man" (Gen. 4:1 NIV, *italics mine)* and Adam did not contradict her. After Abel's death and Seth's birth, she announced, *"God has granted me* another son in the place of Abel" (Gen. 4:25 NIV, *italics mine).*

However, Sarai complained, *"The Lord has kept me* from having children" (Gen. 16:2 NIV, *italics mine).* Luke, the physician, obviously knowledgeable in such matters, reported of Zechariah and Elizabeth, "Both of them were upright in the sight of God, observing all the Lord's commandments blamelessly. *But they had no children"* (Luke 1:6–7 NIV, *italics mine*).

PRINCIPLE 6: *Forgiveness paves the way for new growth.*

David could have insisted on his husbandly rights with Bathsheba, but she willingly gave what he could have taken. She forgave David because she had been forgiven.

We could imagine David's moving out of the palace, being "impeached" as king, even dying, as a result of this incident. Instead we find evidence of new life. And the child David and Bathsheba conceived was special. In fact, "The Lord loved him; and because the Lord loved him, he sent word through Nathan the prophet" (2 Sam. 12:24–25 NIV). The same prophet who had brought God's condemnation to David now informed him of His blessing.

Couples who are forced into marriage by pregnancy often feel tense or "trapped." Yet, sometimes after the birth of a baby who has obvious features of both parents, the family becomes one—unites—*because* of that baby.

In this instance, the birth of the baby paved the way for new growth; for a "second wind" for David and Bathsheba. Isaiah expressed the thought simply, "Forget the former things; do not dwell on the past. See, I am doing a new thing!" (Isa. 43:18–19 NIV).

Tragically those who desperately need "a new thing" in their lives often hold most tenaciously to the remnants of their hurt. They pollute the soil of the new beginning God wants to give them.

The growth of these "forgiveness martyrs" is atrophied because they cannot let go of the past. They choose to lie passively whining or thrashing in the throes of a tantrum in the smoldering, stale ashes of yesterday.

Those who claim martyrdom or demand restitution fail to fully understand forgiveness.

PRINCIPLE 7: *Forgiveness is neither logical nor rational.*

Pastors and evangelists once preached a great deal about restitution or "making the wrongs right." While I believe in restitution as a practical and biblical standard, I suspect that among too many evangelicals it has become a synonym for vengeance—an attempt by the wounded to say to the wounder: "Well, you're not going to get off scot free! You're going to suffer too!" And some want a pound of flesh for an ounce of offense.

Others believe their circumstances so special or spectacular that the normal bounds of forgiveness can be set aside. "If what had happened to me had happened to you, you wouldn't be so forgiving. *I have a right to feel the way I do!*" We also say, "I have to work through this . . .", thus avoiding the decision to forgive.

Those who would not dare to pet a rattlesnake or jump in front of a train or purposely wreck their car fail to understand that unforgiveness is also a terminal choice. Delay is a poisonous venom, however slow-acting.

And even though many wounders have come to conclude that restitution "balances the scales," such an idea violates the following biblical principle.

PRINCIPLE 8: *Forgiveness is never earned.*

Restitution advocates seem to suggest that "After all I've done to make it right, I've *earned* my forgiveness." All of David's eventual accomplishments still did not wipe out the atrocity of his adultery and the murder of an innocent man.

So if you're trying to balance the scales, give up. I've come to discover that forgiveness is a gift. Paul wrote the Ephesians, "For it is by grace you have been saved (forgiven) through faith—and this not from yourselves, it is the gift of God—not of works, so that *no one* can boast" (Eph. 2:9 NIV, *italics mine*).

But sometimes boasting is disguised as testifying or witnessing. The insistence that some have been saved from "deep sin" has influenced young adults to think they must imitate those forgiveness patterns. Sometimes such testimonies become barriers to those who most need to experience the reality of forgiveness, but fear the "wrath of the wounded."

Certainly David paid for his sin: A divided kingdom, a son who had sex with David's concubines on the palace roof before spectators ... painful consequences. And there will always be those who are captivated by another's unhappy consequences. (Haven't we all slowed down and inched by an automobile accident, despite the policeman's gestures to move on?) We've made folk heroes of the executed, and murderers have become household names; their lives, biographical dreams for writers seeking "big bucks."

Paul did not say: "Brothers, forgive as I Paul forgive", but, "Forgive *as the Lord* forgave you" (Col. 3:13 NIV, *italics mine*).

Sometimes we pray: *O Lord, I'm sorry for what happened between 9:15 and 11:45 on Saturday night! It won't happen again,* enthusiastically hoping for an elimination of consequences. One rural preacher spoke of those who "sow their wild oats—then pray for crop failure!"

Often we must pray: *And, give me strength to bear the consequences of my sin.* We must remember that God stands with us during the consequences.

There may be no obvious consequences. We are uniquely designed people, uniquely responsive. The Word carefully points out that "Man looks on the outward appearance, but God looks on the heart" (1 Sam. 16:7 NIV). Sometimes we attempt to appraise another's remorse. But only God knows their internal anguish.

It's easy to quote: "You'll reap what you sow" (Gal. 6:7 NIV), but sometimes in the providence of God, the consequences are postponed or deleted. Such is the wonder of His grace.

PRINCIPLE 9: *Forgiveness is demonstrated.*

It is easy to tell someone how to do something and even easier to do it for him. But sometimes he must be shown. Though God could have: (1) killed David; (2) removed him from his throne, repeating Saul's fate; or (3) "shut up Bathsheba's womb," He didn't do any of these.

The final paragraph of the saga of David and Bathsheba is not found in 2 Samuel, but in Matthew 1. God's forgiveness was demonstrated through David's long life and his son whom the Lord loved. And all of them were in *the lineage of Jesus.*

Lineage was an important issue to the Jews because of their tribal loyalties. Every Jewish child could trace his roots to Father Abraham. The genealogy begins: "Abraham was the father of Isaac, Isaac the father of Jacob, Jacob the father of Judah and his brothers" (Matt. 1:2 NIV).

This is familiar to us after years of Sunday school, vacation Bible schools, and small group Bible studies.

However, if we keep reading, we discover: "Obed (was) the father of Jesse, and Jesse the father of King David" (vv. 5–6). And as we continue: "David was the father of Solomon, whose mother had been Uriah's wife" (v. 6), we feel the need of an exclamation mark! Do you understand what this means? Bathsheba is in Jesus' family tree! David and Bathsheba were the

    great-great-great-great-great
    great-great-great-great-great
    great-great-great-great-great

great-great-great-great-great
great-great-great-great-great-grandparents of
Jesus. And that's *great* news!

"Oh, no!" some may protest. "That can't be true.
Murderers and adulterers in Jesus' family tree?" Yet,
since the Word is infallible and inerrant, I must not
only believe the Word, but accept its promise.

"Coincidence," one woman retorted when I
suggested this reality. "Just a coincidence!" But with
God there is no such thing as coincidence.

Occasionally fathers strongly object to their children's choice of a date, on the basis that the person is
not from the same type of family background. The
possibility of marriage is seen by the father as an invitation to trouble and heartache, and the parent wishes
to protect his child.

If our earthly fathers care that much for us, why
didn't the Heavenly Father care enough to create a
perfect family tree for His Son? Jesus' ancestry included: Judah, who sinned with Tamar (see Matt.
1:3), Rahab, the prostitute (see Matt. 1:5); and Ruth,
a Moabitess from a cursed people (see Matt. 1:5). In
fact, each of the women mentioned in Jesus' family tree
bears a blemished reputation.

Jesus, like every Jew, knew His ancestry. Ancestry
grants no exemptions or deletions. Many who have
scoured their family tree looking for ticketholders on
the *Mayflower* have found a few pirates.

Forgiveness must be demonstrated. God worked
through imperfect people to model the lineage of His
Perfect Son as a monument to forgiveness!

God forgave David and Bathsheba *under the rigidity
of the law,* and He will forgive you under grace. I think
this may have been the point that kept the twelve-year-
old Jesus debating with the "doctors of the law" in the
temple, and which led Charles Wesley to write:

And can it be that I should gain
An interest in the Savior's blood!
   Died He for me, who caused His pain?
   For me, who Him to death pursued?
   Amazing love! How can it be?
   That Thou, my God, shouldst die for me?

Long my imprisoned spirit lay,
Fast bound in sin and nature's night.
Thine eyes diffuse a quickening ray
I woke, the dungeon flamed with light.
My chains fell off; my heart was free.
I rose, went forth, and followed Thee.

Amazing love. How can it be?
That Thou, my God,
Shouldst die for me?

That song has found a niche in the hearts of Christians. Yet daily there are those who sing it, realizing, for the first time, its meaning. Our chains of unforgiveness can fall away, and our hearts can be freed from the burdens.

I recall the night when I heard a strong scholar, Paul Merritt Bassett, explore the genealogy of Jesus. For some time I had been trying to put the pieces together, and that night in a small historic chapel on the campus of Point Loma College in San Diego, the Lord finished the job.

PRINCIPLE 10: *Forgiveness is a promise.*

In understanding the wonder of our salvation, we must recognize the promise of forgiveness.

The promise is so simple that a child can memorize it in a few moments. Unfortunately adults often struggle with it for a lifetime. "If we confess our sins, he is faithful and just and will forgive us our sins and purify us from all unrighteousness" (1 John 1:9 NIV).

The conditions:

1. "If (or when) we confess our sins . . ." When we honestly accept responsibility and confess our sin, He will act in our lives.

2. "He is faithful and just . . ." That compound adjective sounds like a contradiction unless we recall the principle that forgiveness is neither logical nor rational.

3. "He will purify us from all unrighteousness." With Him forgiveness is complete and thorough.

But the process begins with a decision. His decision was first made when He sent the Son; then reaffirmed when He allowed the Son's death.

PRINCIPLE 11: *Forgiveness is a decision!*

Forgiveness is not an abstract ideal we can contemplate—but a reality in which we can participate. You can make a choice, now, to begin or resume your pilgrimage. Billy Graham, through whose ministry millions have come to know the promise of forgiveness, calls his radio program "The Hour of Decision."

"I will arise and go to my father" (Luke 15:18) was a decision.

Will you make that decision to put into practice, through the Lord's help, a dozen principles of forgiveness?

II

Practicing
the Principles

Forgiving:
Myself

Where does forgiveness begin? With me. I deserve to be as forgiving of myself as I am of you.

Because I'm divorced, I struggle with forgiving myself. My wounds are reopened with every reading of Matthew 19 or when people question my authority to minister because of that experience.

Five years after the fact, I'm still trying to determine what caused the divorce. In that sense, I deal daily with forgiveness. Although the proclamation of forgiveness is found in Romans 8:1, "Therefore, there is now no condemnation for those who are in Christ Jesus" (NIV), it's easier for me to quote it to you than to offer myself its comfort.

A similar pillar in the theology of forgiving myself is found in 2 Corinthians 5:17. Paul wrote, "Therefore, if anyone . . ." No, make that more personal:

"Therefore, if Jason Towner is in Christ, he is a new creation; the old has gone; the new has come!" According to this passage, God has reconciled me, Jason Towner, to Himself. Why would God want to do that after what I've done? Because through Christ, He not only forgives but invites me to participate in the ministry of reconciliation. That's like asking a bank robber to become a teller! "We are therefore Christ's ambassadors as though God were making His appeal through us" (2 Cor. 5:20 NIV).

And I've made another discovery. The chapter of Matthew that I find so harsh is preceded by Matthew 18:21–35, in which Jesus' stern words on divorce were preceded by these encouraging words of forgiveness: "How many times shall I forgive my brother when he sins against me? Up to seven times?"

I find hope in Jesus' answer: "Seventy times seven!" I must have used up at least 250 so far.

When I realize—really realize—that God
has forgiven me
is forgiving me
and will continue to forgive me,
I can be more gentle with you and with myself.

And to achieve that forgiving, gentle spirit, there are a number of facts we must accept.

1. Recognize your need for forgiveness.

Examining your own horde of secret sins will probably reveal some long-term items on your agenda of forgiveness, as well as some items that can be resolved only with the help of others.

Sometimes I play a game called "Secrets" with the small children of friends. I ask, "Do you know a secret?" The smallest ones don't, of course, but they often grin because they're not sure and are just learning how to play games of pretend.

Most of them accept my invitation to "Come sit

on my lap while I tell you a secret." And I hold them tight and whisper in their ears, while they giggle or grin or laugh aloud. I whisper to them that they are loved and special.

Then I ask them to "tell me a secret" and sometimes there is only silence. Sometimes they just "buzz-buzz" in my ear. I smile and say, "Oh, but that was a good secret!"

But some know *real* "secrets." And parents have held their breaths, wondering what the child will tell me. For these, "secrets" are not the surprises purchased for a Christmas or birthday—but dark things, coiled, ready to spring, to embarrass and tarnish. Secrets lurk like boogiemen in the quiet corridors of fragile spirits.

Actually in the process of forgiving ourselves, our secrets can be nourished by forgiving others—initiating a rhythm and releasing the energy required for self-forgiveness. "Oh, but you don't know the *me* that I am." No, I don't. But I do know the *me* that I am—and I think my *me* is a lot like your *me*. We're hungry for authentic forgiveness.

Too many of us grew up in a religious culture that systematically depreciated the *me*. Early in life we began receiving signals:

"You're a bad boy!"

"What do you have to say for yourself?"

"Just wait till your father hears about this!"

"Jesus doesn't like little boys who . . ."

"Aren't you ashamed of yourself?"

The organs of our bodies most receptive to emotional sensitivity are our ears.

So I struggle with forgiving myself—my past—my "secrets." And I've discovered that I need your help. I cannot forgive myself without your active participation.

2. Recognize the need to be gentle with yourself and others.

I once viewed some color slides made by a missionary to the Philipines. The slides pictured Filipinos who had beaten themselves in religious rites to atone for their sins, carving dark, bubbly canyons in their backs. Though I was just a boy when I saw them, I've never forgotten those slides.

And though none of us would ever follow such an example of self-inflicted physical damage, we often flog ourselves unmercifully with a mental cat-o-nine-tails, leaving no visible welts, but shredding our delicate spiritual tissue and forming spiritual scar tissue as tough as elephant hide.

Forgiving yourself is a healing, cleansing experience. David pled, "Wash away all my iniquity and cleanse me from my sin" (Ps. 51:2).

I enjoy children's bath times. To watch little ones splashing water and enjoying their favorite toys, and to see the pink glow of soft skin afterward is special.

My mom always hugged me before she lifted me out of the bath. Somehow after a bath, the little fellow who had been so mischievous all day and was now ready for bed, was irresistible. Many times she sang to me or called my name: "Jason . . . I love you." Sometimes the words formed a chant, a melody, a question —but always they were a gentle strum on the strings of my soul.

Long before I knew the word *love*, I knew her embrace. But, I soon grew "too old" to be pampered and was "big enough" to take my own bath. I missed Mom's touch with the washcloth, and still remember it.

But, when I turned my cereal bowl over my head or smeared chocolate pudding all over my face, my mother's patience wore thin. The same washcloth which could give such a loving caress could be wielded like a Brillo pad! Ouch!

In my denomination we have a public altar where people kneel for prayer. That altar has a rich tradition, gathered over the years. The altar is the place for conversion, confession, rededication, marriage, dedication of babies—the significant moments in our lives. In some families, the cycle has gone on for generations. The babies become young adults who return to the same altar where they were baptized to bring their children for baptism.

When someone comes forward to pray, members of the congregation gather around to pray for and with that person. The pray-ers often touch the person. Many embrace each other—one, splashing tears; another, receiving them without embarrassment.

There were times as an adult going through divorce that I wished for someone to hold me, to touch me, to comfort me in that "night season" in which the hours often held more than sixty minutes.

I need someone to kneel with me, to share my tears. When I'm through with myself, I'm exhausted. I need affirmation, healing, forgiveness, cleansing.

But an interesting thing is occurring in churches which use the altar rather than counseling rooms. Traditionally "an altar service" or an invitation was used to close the service.

A few years ago we began developing "the open altar"—a time for members to join the pastor at the altar during his prayer. Gradually we are eliminating the "altar service." Those with spiritual needs come during the open time.

With the open altar, time has become a significant factor. In my background, the congregation was dismissed after the invitation (church membership was conducted at another time), though some people would stay on to pray with a seeker until "he prayed through"—or testified that he had found help.

At the open altar everyone prays alone. There are only a certain number of minutes available; the service must continue!

My friend, Charles Anderson of Calvary Temple in Seattle, has observed, however, that as the altar service has declined, the demand for counseling has increased correspondingly. We need others to help us accept the cleansing reality of forgiveness.

Sometimes we rationalize with the Lord, speaking to Him from the left side of our brains: facts, figures, logical conclusions. But cleansing confession and forgiveness always come from the right side—the side that houses the emotions. David prayed, "Create in me *a clean heart,* O God, and *renew a right spirit within me* . . . Wash me and I will be whiter than snow" (Ps. 51:10, 7 NIV, *italics mine).*

3. Realize that we can't cry over spilled milk!

We've seen enough television police shows to know we have a right to remain silent because "anything you say *can* and *will* be held against you." We understand that. Premature confession or indiscriminate confession can be as bad as confession under duress.

Remember the old movies where the person was brought to jail to hear a crusty old sergeant boast, "I'll make him talk!"? And who could forget Sergeant Friday in "Dragnet"—"Just the facts, ma'am. Just the facts!" And when Perry Mason drilled a lying witness . . .

"You're putting words in my mouth," the witness would protest.

"Nonsense!" would come Perry Mason's retort. "We want the *truth!* Just the truth!"

I've struggled a long time with something that probably should not have happened. When I prayed about it, I kept winking at the Lord with one of those "You know what I mean" kinds of prayers, so I didn't have to *mention* the offense. We all have them in our repertoires.

Finally I drove to Sunset Cliffs off Point Loma in San Diego. The surf pounded furiously against the bluff as it has since time began. I looked around to make certain no one was close enough to hear, and to make sure there wasn't one of those FBI-type snooping "dish" antenna units in an unmarked truck or van parked nearby. I didn't want anyone eavesdropping on that conversation with God.

When I became convinced the great outdoors wasn't bugged, I summoned all my courage and said, *Lord, I want to talk about . . .* and I filled in the blank. The Lord was as anxious for the conversation as I.

I tried tears and explanations, and finally a wrenching confession. By the time the sun set off the California coast, I felt the calm embrace of fresh forgiveness.

God is not a prosecuting attorney. You are! Quit trying to get enough convictions to get re-elected (see Lam. 3:31).

4. Allow God to use your defeats as sandpaper to bring out the grain in your life.

Everything that has happened to you can work for your good—if the right One guides the process.

Though some things I said in a newspaper interview were to be "off the record" (or so I thought), they ended up in an article. My words, taken out of context and inserted as a wrap-up, contradicted what I had said to the conference participants. Some were angry; others, disappointed; most, confused.

Remember the kid who blew bubbles with bubble gum—each one bigger than its predecessor? Remember that confident delight just before the bubble burst? I thought I had "arrived"—to be interviewed by a major daily newspaper, five columns, three inches deep! Well, my bubble burst and I found myself peeling the residue off my face.

I can never call those words back; a retraction would not change the effect of that article.

Once the Lord had my attention, He used my discomfort over the incident to teach me a valuable lesson. And some of those who had the most to say at the time have forgotten about it by now.

Paul wrote, "You ought to forgive and comfort him, so that he will not be overwhelmed by excessive sorrow" (2 Cor. 2:7 NIV). I could only wish they had taken to heart the eighth verse, "Reaffirm your love for him."

5. *Ignore the old photo albums.*

Photo albums of previous failures seldom encourage us; yet, some of us repeatedly turn the pages, reindicting ourselves for yesterday's defeats.

Some of us choose the cycle of defeated living; we know that road without the roadmap. If you're so inclined, take a time-out to ask yourself: "What is in my life at this moment that I will later regret as much as I do this current problem?"

If you're intimidated by yesterday—it's because you decide not to put God's forgiveness to work.

6. *Make forgiving yourself a full-time commitment.*

Forgiveness must be a full-time commitment, not "moonlighting." I need forgiveness. I need to be a forgiver and a cheerleader for those who are out there on the field taking their licks. These may be good times for me, but somewhere a brother struggles under his load.

If the Lord has forgiven Jason Towner, who is Jason Towner to reject such forgiveness by not forgiving himself? If the Lord has forgiven _____ (insert your name), who are you to reject or limit that forgiveness?

Before you can finally forgive yourself, however, you have to turn in *all* your claim checks for martyrdom. You cannot keep a single one.

The athlete who wishes to compete in the Boston Marathon does not simply tie his track shoes and ask: "Which way to the starting line?" He trains strenuously to prepare for competition. With forgiveness, too, we are always in training.

7. Don't accept a substitute for authentic forgiveness.

Ever see those Las Vegas marquees that blaze brilliantly twenty-four hours a day? Well, I have had a billboard in my spirit that flashes one message: Failure! Failure!

To me, divorce has always been spelled F-A-I-L-U-R-E! Just before Jane moved out, I heard a pastor "pull out all the stops" in a sermon with the thesis: No matter how successful you are otherwise, if you fail at home, you are a *real failure!*

Sometimes after a conference or speaking engagement, unable to fall asleep, I still find myself staring through the darkness at that blinking, pulsating sign: *You're a failure! You're a failure!*

Every time I've published an article or book, I have walked past that marquee, waving the proof of my success. Yet the lights still blinked on.

So I began to try to write to win friends and influence people. My only credentials as a writer come from you, the reader, through your decision to read my work. My temptation is to use you, the reader, to stroke my sagging ego. My temptation is to use your recognition of me as author or speaker to get an even larger photo or larger, bolder type in my next brochure or poster. *My temptation is to use outward signs of success as compensation for my inner feelings of failure.*

Keith Miller has offered me an alternative to continuing to view that flashing "Failure!" message: *Don't pay the bill!* Then the electricity will be cut off. I have tried to take that advice by forgiving myself my shortcomings. The marquee lights are becoming dim.

8. Let go and let God . . .

Sometimes I'm so busy trying to manage my own forgiveness needs that I don't leave room for God to work. Tragically many of us have experienced not the heartbreak of psoriasis, but the failure of forgiveness. Somehow we can't fully grasp the reality of forgiveness, and become bound to the past.

This process is "emotional archeology"—digging up the past, sifting through the garbage, looking for previously unexplored details and angles. That is at the heart of most struggles with forgiving ourselves.

Recently I spoke on intimacy at a college in Boston. A young woman came up after the lecture and asked, "How do you *know for sure* that you have been forgiven? My boyfriend wants to know if I am a virgin." She looked away significantly.

"And you're afraid you'll lose him if you tell the truth?" I asked. Her tears were an eloquent answer to my question.

"Well, if it isn't a problem for your Brother," I said, "it shouldn't be a problem for your boyfriend."

"I don't have a brother," she sobbed.

"Sure you do. His name is Jesus. The Word says that we are heirs and joint heirs with Him. He's my Brother *and* your Brother. If you've asked Jesus to forgive you, you're pure in His sight. Who are you to question His judgment?"

Although her tears continued, their origin changed from remorse to joy.

Most of us can never be "pure in history." So, the Lord calls us to be "pure in heart."

Once I was bound by sin's galling fetters (and
   memories)
Chained like a slave, I struggled in vain (to forgive
   myself)
But I received a glorious freedom
When Jesus broke my fetters in twain.

Freedom from fear with all of its torments
Freedom from care with all of its pain
Freedom in Christ, my blessed Redeemer
He who has rent my fetters in twain.

Glorious freedom! Wonderful freedom!
No more in chains of sin I repine
Jesus the glorious Emancipator
Now and forever
He shall be mine!

Forgiveness liberates us from the tyranny of yesterday's sins and failures. We are more than products
of our past. We are pilgrims in forgiveness.

Perhaps you've watched too many sunsets and
sunrises without the fresh reality of forgiveness. But
there can come those dawning moments when we are
so anxious for the sunrise that our hearts almost burst.
There is One who waits in those dawns.

God goes before us to prepare our hearts to receive the confirmation of forgiveness. Sometimes we
can't see the forest for the trees. That was John's
premise when he said: "This is how we set our hearts
at rest in His presence, whenever our hearts condemn
us, For God is greater than our hearts and he knows
everything" (1 John 3:16 NIV).

Ruth, the Moabitess widow, gave up her claim
checks to a second marriage in Moab, to accompany
her mother-in-law, Naomi, back to Judah. She blis-
tered her hands and forehead in the merciless sun,
harvesting barely enough grain to feed the two of

them. And the dawn always came too soon. She was still exhausted from the previous day when Naomi awakened her.

But on the dawn of her wedding to Boaz—
> On the dawn of Obed's birth
> On the dawn of her grandson's coronation as King of Israel,
She did not look to the past!

If God loved Ruth that much, how much does He love me? Paul declared that the One *"who began a good work in you* will carry it on to completion until the day of Christ Jesus" (Phil. 1:6 NIV).

"If any one (including Jason Towner) be in Christ, he is a new creation."

I am forgiven! That is as real as any physical law of the universe. He who was under no obligation to forgive me, has forgiven me *and* offers me numerous opportunities to participate in the ministry of forgiveness and reconciliation (see Col. 1:13).

But first, I must forgive myself, my weaknesses, my inferiorities.

That is always a decision—not an emotion.

Forgiving:
The Ex

I saved this chapter until last to write, though it does not appear as Chapter Fourteen in this book. In fact, I wrote it only after my editor, Ann Severance, asked for it! She had looked for it as soon as the manuscript arrived on her desk.

Actually something occurred which assured me that I was ready to attempt this chapter. I will not share the details, except to say I had an encounter with my ex-wife. This should have been the perfect opportunity to pull out those well-rehearsed-but-stored-for-such-a-moment-as-this/prerecorded-for-this-time-zone lines, but I didn't use them.

Rather, I listened while she talked.

Later, jogging through the cold on Christmas morning, there came the slightest warming glow from deep within. The "unfinished" was, in fact, finished! The unexpected had happened. Deep within my spirit—I heard the bells on Christmas Day.

You say, "Oh, sure, that's easy for you, Mr. Jason Towner, writer, speaker, professional single—divorce made you who you are (and by the way, *Who do you think you are anyway?*). You've profited from your hurt!"

O.K., I'll admit only that my hurt provided the fire by which the skilled craftsman shapes the steel. I didn't like the fire and I didn't like the pounding I received on the anvil. But had that trauma not occurred, my writing would still be in shoe boxes in the closet, and I certainly would not be planning to fly across the country Christmas night to a speaking engagement.

It would have been easy for me to have tackled *Jason Hates Jane and Wants to Get Even*—but plenty of other folks could write that kind of book.

For me, forgiving my ex has not been a hurdle or a hassle—perhaps because of the strength of my love for her, a love which still occupies a quiet place in my heart. I've listened skeptically to those who have tried to convince me their love "died" or was amputated at a precise moment.

Recently, a friend of mine in California had radical cancer surgery. I called a couple of days after the surgery to express my concern. Across 2,000 miles we shared our faith.

"Too bad about the cancer . . . I wish I knew how to help . . ." was about all I could say.

"They tell me I've had it for a year," he said. But his next words stopped me cold: "And the emotional cancer has been there years longer than that!"

"The emotional cancer . . ." those words echoed long after the conversation ended . . . still at midnight . . . at 6:00 A.M. the next morning.

But for the grace of God . . . hatred, like a malignancy, could still be growing somewhere inside me. The poison of unfinished business explains much illness. Physicians warn us that repressed emotions can be hazardous to our health. My friend is positive proof!

When Jane left, I struggled for a strategy to get her back. I pleaded, I prayed, I petitioned. Eventually I learned that the midnight calls and "Please come homes" were only tearing *me* apart.

My doctor found that I had a heart problem—a discrepancy in the left mitral valve. My being seventy pounds overweight and under intense emotional pressure must have contributed to my health problems.

After carefully rehearsing my presentation, I shared the discovery with Jane. No lawyer arguing a capital offense before a jury was ever better prepared.

"Jane, I'm falling apart without you."

But that strategy failed—as did the others.

Fortunately a Polish track coach; Robert Schuller's book, *You Can Become the Person You Want to Be;* and a group of compassionate friends too numerous to mention were orchestrated by the Holy Spirit to terminate such thinking and plotting. Today, there's nothing wrong with my heart physiologically or emotionally. If I ever did have a broken heart, I have survived.

Some have suggested, "You're not over Jane." I am surprised by the number of people who believe that someway, someday, we'll get back together and live "happily ever after" and write a best seller.

But at least I can use her name. I have met people who can't, substituting "ex" or "her" or "him."

To forgive one with whom you have stood naked
or shared an heirloom blanket on a cold night
or dreamed dreams
or split the last piece of dessert
or traded Christmas surprises
is still a decision.

The "innocent victims" stroke their hatred and anger and resentment as they would a prized Angora cat—yet deny such emotions exist. The mantle of the "innocent victim" can be a suffocating shroud that shuts out the freshness of future.

I have a friend who fumes because her ex drives a new Cadillac every year while she rambles around in a battered VW with a lien.

And another friend squandered his assets so his ex-wife wouldn't have anything to collect, despite the court order.

And I read an account of a man who took literally the court's order to give his wife half the house. With a chain saw he cut the house in two!

> And I know that your ex may owe you a bushel of
>   alimony,
> or may harass you,
> or make promises to the kids he won't keep.
> And you have had to pay for the braces,
> and you have to one-up him on birthdays and
>   Christmas,
> while he runs you down to the children.
> And he is not hurting as much as you are . . . .

Job didn't have all the answers—and neither do I. The only universal feature of life is that *everyone* gets sixty seconds per minute—not fifty-nine or sixty-one, but sixty. That's why the Word tells us the story of Hosea and Gomer, and why Jesus commented on forgiving seventy times seven.

How do you forgive your ex?

1. Start by recognizing the big things that bug you; then list all of the minor ones.

Go ahead! Be sure you get down everything. I'm no prude, just a pilgrim. I'll go first:

- I resented being forced to accept the standard of celibacy.
- I resented doing the laundry.
- I resented cooking and eating alone.
- I resented the conspicuous silence in the small church I attended.
- I resented the Kentucky Fried Chicken box lunches I ate on a hundred Sunday afternoons as much as I resented the people who never invited me home with them for a meal.

Jane was not the cause of most of my complaints. But it was easier to blame her than to confront my real feelings. How many of the complaints on your list can you or your ex solve?

You'll never get even, and trying isn't worth the price.

2. *Tithe your problems.* Give God all possible complaints at this particular moment and promise that as He deals with them, you'll turn over more and more to Him.

3. *Forgive on the spot.* When the videotape plays and you feel pressure rising, ask God to help. As you sit in church or a dentist's chair; as you wait stuck in traffic or to cash a check or mail a letter, the enemy will trot out all sorts of videos for your review. That may be all it will take to send your emotional Dow-Jones plummeting.

In *Jason Loves Jane* I related the story of the 4:00 A.M. "wide-awake" video theaters of the mind, when it was tempting to think (in hindsight) of "what I should have done."

If that moment comes, don't rewind it for another look and please don't put it into slow motion or instant stop. If you do, you plant a seed for a distant harvest!

4. *Don't reenact old battles.* I sat in a chain hamburger emporium the other day listening as a verteran

relived battles from World War II. All I wanted to do was munch my hamburger in peace, but I tried to listen politely.

But there are as many veterans of Domestic Wars and as many emotionally disabled vets as Veterans of Foreign Wars that march in the parades on Memorial Day. And they don't get special license plates.

I know unfaithfulness is hard to forgive . . .

I know that feeling of foolishness when realizing suddenly "something has been going on" . . .

I know the feeling when the money is gone and there are still days left in the month . . .

I know what it is to watch your ex prosper . . .

But, we are called to follow the Forgiver, to participate at His invitation in His work, to forgive as He has forgiven us (see Col. 3:13).

So when your ex buys a new car or a new house or remarries or spends money on himself while your children do without, it's hard to say, *Lord, I commit this to You.*

When your VW breaks down and has to be towed in and your seven-year-old reports on his recent ride in Dad's new car, it's hard to say, *Lord, I commit this to You.*

When you realize that your *ex* is still loved by the Lord—your ex, the one you once promised to love forever—it's hard to say, *Lord, I commit this to You.*

Some time ago a woman in a divorce workshop admitted she was having a tough time accepting this idea. She had been divorced the year before. Her husband had asked for his freedom, assuring her, "There isn't another woman." He was divorced barely three months before he remarried. And she had thought he would come back to *her!*

The lady complained, "The first thing they did as a couple was to 'hit the altar,'" meaning, they rededicated their lives. I will never forget her words, "How could He do that to me?" At the time I did not realize the woman was referring to the Lord, not to her former husband. She was really asking, "How could Jesus forgive them so easily after what they did to me?"

When I understood that, I was better able to counsel her.

That night, in a lodge in McCall, Idaho, we put a chair in the center of our group. If anyone needed help, all they had to do was to sit in the chair while Christian friends would gather around them, touching them and praying.

As several came to sit in the chair, I asked: "What do you want the Lord to do for you?"

They stated their needs. For some, the preliminary recitations and side roads took awhile. I would reply, "I wish I could help you." Their shock often registered on their faces.

"*I* can't help you . . . but God can. Let's pray."

Some were able to leave burdens in McCall.

So that brings me to you. What do you want the Lord to do for you, my friend, my skeptical reader?

Forgiveness is not a feeling or an emotion; it is always a decision. "Inasmuch as ye have done it unto one of the least of these my brethren, ye have done it unto me" (Matt. 25:40). Have you made your ex one of "the least"? The Towner version reads, "Inasmuch as you have *forgiven* the least of these, you have done it to me."

The moment of confrontation of review of that which you have chosen not to forgive will come. Count on it!

Three years ago, at a Christian Writers' Conference led by Sherwood Wirt, I found the opportunity to experience an afterglow. It was to be held after the session on the rocks in front of the organ chapel. So I decided to go *observe*. I found myself seated on a rock in a circle of other writers, on a night beyond belief—crisp, with a million stars strung for the occasion and the sound of water rushing through the stream far below. There was a conspicuous absence of the sounds common to American life—TV, radios, cars, sirens, trucks, jets, air conditioners, vacuum sweepers—just the flute-like sounds of night were heard.

Dr. Wirt explained the groundwork. Each person would give his name and tell what he wanted the Lord to do for him. However, if he did not wish prayer, he could merely say, "Praise the Lord," and we would move on to the next person.

To my surprise, mine was the first name called. My temptation was to just give my name and then say, "Praise the Lord!"

But those words stepped aside so that I could confess my need. I knelt in the rock bed and others gathered around me and began praying.

Dr. Wirt let me pray and the group prayed. Finally he asked me to repeat: *Lord, put me on a cross . . . and crucify me. . . .* Well, that's not the way members of my denomination pray; that is not our terminology, our process.

But the prayer flowed. There was a sense of peace, of quiet and joy that exploded like a sunburst. I surrendered the seeds of resentment that I had planted, fertilized, and watered, while waiting for them to break through the soil.

That night will always be a special one for me.

One year later, I returned to those rocks for another afterglow, eventually wandering off to stand overlooking the mountain lake in that incredible cathedral.

Again I asked the Lord to remove seeds, ordered from scattered catalogs, in my belief that they would make a garden.

Mighty oaks from little acorns grow! So it is with the human spirit. Small resentments can grow into full-grown unforgiveness.

Forgiveness is always a decision.

Perhaps this is your season of decision. Could I invite you to take a moment to check the inventory?

Forgiving:
The Church

"Look, I know how to forgive people and even how to help other people forgive," the young minister said. "But how do I forgive the *church?*"

The church, the institution most committed to forgiveness, ordained to be the community of the forgiven and the *forgiving*, has frequently been a setting for border skirmishes, feuds, battles, and open guerilla warfare. Only the Lord knows how many people have been crushed in the bureaucratic machinery of institutional politics.

In the closets of many a church and religious institution are a lot of skeletons. The institution that the Lord established to promote His kingdom often fails to recognize or respond to human needs. Sometimes its bulk prohibits its moving quickly and efficiently to touch those who hurt. But we expect it to

71

respond to us at a moment's notice. Somehow despite our own organized committees, task forces, offices, divisions, departments, and priorities, people—our most precious resource, those we are "to save"—often get lost in the machinery.

Thousands of religious technicians and theocrats are required to keep the great machines of denominational structures and independent ministries turning (some would say that *spinning* is a far more accurate term.) Some of those church bureaucrats have become most unresponsive to the grass-roots element. Just as laborers occasionally are mangled by machinery, so there are sensitive individuals (and their families) who become victims of "church politics" and intrigue. Simply stated, if there are winners, there have to be losers! The stakes are high.

1. We must recognize that "church politics" are not new. The bitter dispute between Paul and Barnabas, which caused them to decide that they could not work together, arose over a fellow worker (see Acts 15:36–41). The test of strength between Jews and Gentiles over the issue of circumcision was well-known, as was a dispute over the treatment of widows (see Acts 6:1). And factions in the Corinthian church were notable. Some followed Paul; some, Apollos; and some, Cephas (see 1 Cor. 1:12, NIV).

While we protest today's church politics, we must recognize the inevitable recurrence of some of the same mistakes that brought reproach on the first followers of Christ. Should two thousand years of practice as the church not have taught us something?

Church fights and splits often evolve from the same factors that lead to divorce—fragility of ego or hardness of hearts (see Matt. 19:8).

Sometimes the issues and loyalties are perpetuated and encouraged by ingrown leadership suffering from "hardening of attitude." When the arteries of the church are clogged and narrowed, fresh blood cannot be absorbed into its lifestream; therefore, some parts suffer malnutrition.

I meet a lot of people who are angry with the church—meaning: sometimes, a denomination; sometimes, all evangelicals; and sometimes, the congregation on the corner of Seventeenth Street and Melrose. And I struggle with the casualties of our uncompassionate bureaucracy—with the wounded victims of an ecclesiastical machinery that does not always understand or tolerate the individual—one which seeks to tool-and-die those who would serve through its ministries.

Some of our most creative minds have been ostracized or demoted while others, less qualified, but with an understanding of the workings of the political system, have climbed to leadership posts and positions of influence, encumbered with a backpack of I.O.U.'s, and hoarse from the chorus of yeses volunteered en route.

Situations are seldom as simple as they seem. Certainly there are those who are frightened by new thinking, by mavericks. Leaders frequently use the term *loyalty* as if it were synonymous with *commitment*. But *blind loyalty* means the cadre sit quietly by, letting others do their thinking, choosing never to rise to the defense of a colleague, or to protest a policy burdened by a hidden agenda.

The church's current diet of internal politics denies the nutrients needed for mere survival, let alone growth.

This may partially explain the enormous growth of the electronic church. Viewers, many of whom are casualties of the local church, wish to be far removed from political skirmishes masqueraded in doctrinal or biblical interpretation. The electronic church allows us to sit in the safety of our living rooms or dens as spectators, reaching for our checkbooks to make a contribution, if we are so moved.

2. We must realize that the willingness to forgive naturally involves the risk that the offending sin may recur.

Forgiveness allows room for history to repeat itself. That reality often causes negative people to conclude: "Then I'll never be vulnerable again." So they surround themselves with a transparent shield, which repulses the most harmful or stressful attacks, but also limits growth within its confines.

For example, John has not forgiven the congregation that voted his father out as senior minister after a major conflict over relocation. How could he easily forget the experience of sitting with his teen-age friends and hearing the vote announced to the congregation? He realized that some of his friends' parents must have voted against his dad.

He also remembered the subdued quiet in the parsonage that day and in succeeding weeks as his parents struggled with the realities of the decision. He recalls the equal restraint of the farewell reception. In ten years, John's father had given much to that church. How could the people do this to him and to his family?

So John has rejected the church. How does he know that his father will not be voted out of another congregation? "If that is what the church is all about, who needs it?" And many children of ministers will nod in agreement from their self-imposed exiles. Some have rebelled against the congregation's expectations of the pastor's child—a double standard which was often unrealistic.

3. We must recognize that the church must deal with problems for which it is not always equipped or trained.

A pastor disappointed Herman twenty-five years ago—and he hasn't been back to church since. Our unrealistic expectations of a minister—placing him on a pedestal because of his "calling"—cause us to be angry when he disappoints or fails us. Some ministers burn out trying to imitate the model superpastor. We expect the minister to be teacher-manager-pulpiteer-counselor-home/hospital visitor-cheerer-upper-administrator-financial genius-promotional specialist. Just when is there time to be a husband and father?

The problem will intensify. Congregations want the superchurch, their expectations fueled by the perfect models they see every Sunday morning on television. In those video churches, no one ever sings off-key or forgets the words—and the minister always finishes on time.

What if the commandment read: "Thou shalt not covet thy neighbor's church or its ministries or its prestige"?

The explosive growth of the electronic church has inevitably whetted the appetite of those who seek to imitate on a scaled-down version that which they cannot attain. As inflation continues to escalate, the financial pinch of the people of God becomes more obvious. Thus, the budget becomes another arena in the continuing battle for power and influence. Control of the purse strings means control of the church.

4. We must forgive the church's inappropriate responses.

When the church responds in silence, we must forgive that silence.

When the church responds with platitudes, prooftexts, or memorized Scripture quoted without real feeling, we must forgive those responses.

And, when the church forces some to wait in quiet, steaming hells while policy is debated, we must forgive that procrastination.

Sally has served in every possible leadership position for eighteen years. The Sunday morning after her husband moved out of their home and in with his girl friend, Sally went through her traditional routine: reviewing her Sunday school lesson and getting the kids up, fed, and dressed for church.

Later, as she walked down the hall of the educational building toward her classroom, she felt tears begin to form. She knew it would be difficult to face her class that day. How many of her pupils already knew? *Lord, help me,* she prayed as she walked.

When she neared the classroom, the minister of the church blocked her path. Her heart skipped a beat. *Did he know? How could he not know?* Fred had been involved in affairs before.

The pastor intercepted her.

"Sally," he said in what she considered a stained-glass voice, "the educational committee met last night. And we think it would be best if you didn't teach, er, well . . . until this is all settled. I've asked Jim Martin to teach the class for you. I'm sure you understand." And he turned and hurried away, his last words still hanging in the air.

Sally could hardly see through the flood of tears that, at that moment, evacuated her reservoir. Hearing footsteps, she quickly ducked into the women's restroom, to hide in one of the stalls. Halfway through the Sunday school hour, she slipped out and drove to a nearby park to cry until noon. *How could my church reject me, too?* she asked.

Sally is not the Lone Ranger. Many victims of divorce:

- have been asked to resign their positions of leadership immediately
- have *not* been asked to serve after their term expired

- were given cool receptions in social settings
- were angered or alienated by the judgmental attitudes of some leaders.

The silence merely broke the spirits of others. If Sally had lost her husband through death, there would have been casseroles and pies, sympathy cards, floral arrangements, visits from the pastoral staff, a prayer from the pulpit, a notice in the church newsletter.

But divorce is different. "We don't know what to say." So some quietly take their places outside the church, while others cannot resist the temptation to pelt the church with verbal rocks.

We have made room in the church for the embezzler, the harlot, the murderer. But how much room is reserved in the pew for the divorced?

Do we self-righteously distribute spiritual merit badges to those who have stuck it out in dead-end marriages, while condemning those who have been forced to choose divorce?

5. *We must avoid the temptation to say, "I told you so!"* It takes enormous discipline to stifle a smile when the smug confident Christian who ignored our need is suddenly desperate; when your *yesterday* is their *today*. The words, "Now you know how I felt!" perch on the tips of our tongues, poised for those moments.

Some of our brothers and sisters have not received gentle care despite Paul's admonition in Galatians 6:1: "Brothers, if someone is caught in sin, you who are spiritual should restore him gently" (NIV). Certainly it is clear that the early church faced real problems— "the sexually immoral . . . idolaters . . . adulterers . . . male prostitutes . . . homosexual offenders . . . thieves . . . the greedy . . . drunkards . . . slanderers . . . swindlers . . . And that is what some of you were" (1 Cor. 6:10–11 NIV)—and so must we.

No sin is smaller or greater than another. It does not take God longer to forgive some sins than to forgive others: One-tenth of a second for lying; two seconds for adultery, etc.

If the church is the model for forgiveness, we can avoid uncomfortable situations by remaining calm, and by ignoring the witch hunt for those who do not fit the conventional molds.

6. *We must realize that rejection from one church or one congregation is not final.* Part of the forgiving process may be beginning again ... moving on. Sometimes the painful and difficult circumstances that lead us to change church affiliation provide new growth.

I have a friend who won't attend church because, in her judgment, "It's full of hypocrites."

I've so often been tempted to respond: "Oh, go ahead—one more can't hurt."

And so her Christian witness shrinks day by day. Perhaps if she were able to find a congregation with whom she feels compatible and with whom she could conscientiously worship, she would stretch and grow in spirit.

7. *We must realize that we are the church.* To forgive the church is to forgive ourselves. In analyzing our need, we have overlooked those who see us as "the church" and now rehearse similar complaints against us.

To forgive the church is to plant the seeds that may blossom
—when we weep
—when our burdens must be shared
—when we rejoice in our triumphs.
Some of us become "the perishing" in need of rescue:

> Down in the human heart
> crushed by the tempter;

Feelings lie buried
  that grace can restore.
Touched by a loving heart
  wakened by kindness
Chords that are broken
  will vibrate once more.

The children of Israel did not develop their identity overnight, but through a series of stretching experiences—exile, captivity, famine, pestilence, war, internal dissension.

So it is with the church. A careful reading of the Old Testament reports the failings of the priests and the bureaucratic over-development of the Jewish religion. But throughout those pages is the overwhelming theme of the love of Jehovah for his people.

The church is called to be the celebrating modeler of forgiveness, a witness to a skeptical world desperately craving authentic forgiveness. Naturally the Enemy would seek to discredit the model. And often we provide ample raw materials with which he can ignite the flames of discontent.

If the church could become a community of the *forgiven* (past tense) and the *forgiving* (present tense), we would find that same flame which singed the church at Pentecost, ready to rebaptize us today.

Forgiving the church is a decision—and sometimes a tough one.

Forgiving:
Parents

Where were you on May 4, 1960? You probably can't remember. But at least one adult remembers every detail of that day, having watched the reruns of the incident in the theater of her mind at least once a week.

In twenty years, this victim has not spoken to her mother. She has ignored: Her mother's birthday
the death of her father
twenty Mother's Days
and twenty year-end versions of "Auld Lang Syne."

The event has been caged, fed, and groomed like a panther in a zoo, so well-nourished, in fact, that it has outgrown its cage.

This obsession has sapped her strength, taxed her nerves, weakened her health, and destroyed her marriage. Somehow she thought by carrying this cross,

she would eventually repay her mother for failing her when she needed help.

What does the daughter want:

Her mother's hide mounted on the den wall?

Her mother caught in some embarrassing scenario to balance the scale—to erase the past twenty years?

Her unforgiveness has forever confined the young woman to the role of a child, like a retarded daughter who has been placed in an institution. She does not realize that she alone has the key to her cell.

At this point you may ask, "Why doesn't God do something about this?"

God has. He has worked with the resources at His disposal—a heartbroken mother who has bitten her lip as she watched the reruns of her mistake.

But what the daughter does not know is that her mother's brokenness became God's means to making her a twentieth-century saint

who never meets a stranger

who leads many to the Lord

who befriends thousands

and whose infectious smile brightens the day

for many pilgrims.

Ironically many have plotted their future to be like this lady—a friend of God. They do not know that her broken heart has produced her saintly nature—and has made a beautiful mosaic of a broken life!

Perhaps the mother's prayer will be answered and the prodigal daughter will come home. On how many afternoons has she stood and prayed to the God who created the oceans to quiet the surf within her daughter's soul?

In my own mind I believe that the miracle, if it comes, will come long after the mother is gone—after the daughter has claimed victory. And she will discover, in the absence of grief, her own defeat!

So the picture of a beautiful young woman sits with four others, on a piano. All but one of the photos is recent. But there is no indication of rank as the mother explains: "This is my oldest son John, who is a pilot. And my daughter Ellen, who is a teacher in Texas . . . and this is my daughter Becky . . ."

No, there is no pause
no crack in the voice . . .
But there are those times during the telephone commercials ("Reach out and touch someone . . .") that the break comes. She excuses herself from the room for a moment.

That's all it would take—a ringing telephone and the words: "I wanted to call you and say I'm sorry."

The Christmas season prompts the hope that "this could be the year" for five children to stand around the piano once more, singing "Silent Night," as they did Christmas Eve, 1959.

Although the other children have given up hope, the mother still believes. Again, she will make her daughter's favorite Christmas cookies—*just in case* "this is the year."

And on New Year's Eve, the mother will again act surprised: "Look what I just found on the top shelf! I must have overlooked them . . . Christmas macaroons. Have some, won't you?"

I wish there were some way I could locate this daughter. Many nights, her mother has supplied my need for a friend or for someone to call my name in prayer. I hope this chapter may have a part in filling her need to reach her daughter.

Maybe this daughter will read this, and for one moment, think about Christmas macaroons. Will she remember that she was always the first one in the family to have one?

Will she remember how her mother would stand there waiting to hear the inevitable, "Can I have another one?"

"That good, huh?"

"I'll need to taste another one before I can say for sure."

What about it, daughter? Today would be a good day to forgive your mother; she forgave you a long time ago!

The first and most significant item on the agenda of adulthood is forgiving one's parents. The only way one can escape childhood and get on with the business of adulthood is to confront that concern.

Many adults choose to suppress the unforgiven areas, reporting: "My parents were super, wonderful, great, etc." Within their memories, however, lurks a stern, forbidding authority figure.

"Honor your father and mother, so that you may live long in the land the Lord your God is giving you" (Exod. 20:12 NIV). This, along with some other expressions, some biblical—some quasi-biblical—form common admonitions to children:

"This hurts me more than it hurts you" (to which I always wanted to reply, "Oh, yeah?").

"Spare the rod and spoil the child!"

"After *all* I've done for you."

"I don't want to hear another word."

There are phrases which wound like a bullet. And long after parents and children make up, the words still ricochet through the corridors of the mind.

Most of us have heard such expressions on more than one occasion; some have made them second- or third-generation clichés. Other phrases may bring back memories which cause a smile.

Children are wounded through mental or spiritual abuse—with no bruises or broken bones, only broken spirits—and that's hard evidence for a court to ponder. Some children carry their soul-scars to the grave.

Years ago, when I was working as an embalmer, a sight was etched permanently into my mind. Two babies lay on embalming tables rather than snugly and confidently in their mother's arms. One had been in an automobile accident; the other, starved to death. That afternoon made me doubt my pursuit of a career as a funeral director.

How could God let a tiny, innocent baby starve to death at the hands of negligent parents? Hadn't God heard its cries in the night? How could He "allow" the parents to survive? Why didn't He take them? My anger was compounded when an "understanding" judge let them off with only a slap on the wrist and two years' probation.

Now, years later, my anger has cooled. I believe that God, in that very moment of my protest, called out across the playgrounds of heaven and summoned that child into His presence. And for a moment, the Lord held that squirming, giggling child and whispered, "I love you."

With that thought, Psalm 21:4 makes far more sense, "He asked you for life, and you gave it to him—length of days, forever and ever" (NIV). That child will forever know the Father's love, free from child abuse.

What would have happened had that child lived to confront even more pain and indignity? Whose Sunday school class would he have terrorized? How would he have fought back? Would he have abused *his* children?

I am convinced that adults must grant amnesty to their parents. That does not excuse their action, but puts them into the perspective of forgiveness.

Take my friend Dana—a beautiful woman who "can't" go home again. In the era of women's liberation, she's a prodigal daughter, the years of her rebellion acting as sandpaper on her sensitive spirit.

The cards she sends on birthdays and at Christmas contain beautiful messages, but the sentiment is not there. For a time, Dana shopped for hours for cards that said *only* what she wanted them to say, wishing the pretty words of the message could really be hers. And her rare times at "home" comprise the least possible amount of time.

This chapter is difficult for me to write. I'm still working on some of the concepts.

I used to watch "Leave it to Beaver" and covet the relationship between Mr. and Mrs. Cleaver and their sons. And Robert Young in "Father Knows Best" always did seem to "know best."

I know that my parents love me and have always loved me. But my dad never *told* me until the day before his recent heart surgery. I grew into adulthood desperately needing to hear those words, "I love you." Certainly he has acknowledged that he is "proud of me" but that is not necessarily synonymous with love. There is a generation of men who covet these words, yet cannot break the mold with their own sons.

But I've always had to struggle with my dad and his high expectations. It didn't matter what other kids did, I was *expected* to behave or face *immediate* physical consequences. My dad took discipline seriously. There was none of that "Just wait till I get you home" stuff.

As a child, I was embarrassed by the fact that my dad was the church janitor. Back in those days when we were "on the other side of the tracks" economically, our church was painfully plain; the plainer, the more spiritual. Yet to my dad that building was a sacred trust—it was where the Lord met His people. And my dad went about that job with incredible devotion.

There was that time my brother and I got caught sliding our ample bottoms across the altar rail. Boy, did we get to see the inside of the boiler room quickly! That day, my dad spared us the "this hurts me more than it hurts you" routine.

But in fact, it *did* hurt him—because to him, the altar was a precious place.

To pacify restless children during our long church services, many parents excused them to go outside and play. But we stayed till the service's end because my dad had to lock up afterward. On more than one occasion, my dad carried a sleeping boy to the car.

So very early in my life I confronted "peer pressure"—trying to be liked even though I was the "tough guy's son."

There is no shortage of tension between children and parents. On more than one occasion, after being punished, I muttered, "Just wait till I get big." That almost always resulted in: "What did you say, young man?" and a speedy round two of punishment. Finally I learned to keep my mouth shut. I mastered the skill of confining my anger to my heart!

A lot of adults never empty the reservoir of unresolved anger, stored since childhood, and particularly degenerative to the delicate surfaces of a child's spirit.

Most parents rely on the model of parenting their parents provided, with certain modifications. I have come to realize that my dad has acted toward me in much the same way his father acted toward him. Therefore I must conclude my father did the best he could. I cannot hold my father responsible for his lack of knowledge concerning recent developments in child psychology.

After all, parenting often comes with "no previous experience," and no one has ever been disqualified for lack of experience. Yet only a small percentage of successful parenting is biological; most is emotional.

Okay, suppose your parents failed you. Why not forgive them? Turn in all your claim checks—it's possible to apply that toward a good relationship: parent/adult to son-daughter/adult.

There are those adults who have not known the luxuries of receiving good parenting, but who have decided not to let that prevent or limit their success as parents.

Perhaps you were adopted. Many adults insist on launching an expedition into their roots, trying to find the biological parent who gave them up for adoption. Some will even ask courts to "undo" the damage.

One friend made a choice *not* to pursue the biological secrets. He decided to accept the parents who have stood with him across the years. Art Linkletter, who was adopted by a Methodist minister, noted, "It only takes a moment to be a biological parent; but it takes a lifetime to be an authentic parent."

So you may need to forgive that mystery parent without ever understanding "Why?" they gave you up.

Well, now it's your turn—

What bugs you about your parents?

1. Parents who play favorites. That's more common that we like to admit; some parents do not love their children equally. And the problem is certainly not new.

"Isaac spoke to his son Esau" while Rebekah spoke "to her son Jacob" (Gen. 27:5–6 NIV). When Rebekah learned that Isaac had requested Esau to prepare his favorite meal, she spun a plan to deceive Isaac into blessing his second-born (and her favorite) son, Jacob.

Afterward, Esau made "loud and bitter" protests,

but it was too late. When Rebekah learned that Esau planned to kill Jacob in revenge, she said to her son, "Flee at once to my brother Laban in Haran. Stay with him a while until your brother's fury subsides. When *your brother* is no longer angry with you and forgets *what you did to him* . . ." (Gen. 27:43–45 NIV, *italics mine*). How conveniently she excused her own involvement!

Apparently the tendency to "play favorites" was passed on to the next generation. Ten chapters later, the writer reports that when Joseph's "brothers saw that their father loved him more than any of them, they hated him and could not speak a kind word to him" (Gen. 37:4 NIV).

Parents still play favorites, although most would strongly protest that they treat all of their children alike.

Sometimes the favoritism (and antagonism) is nourished by a child's behavior. Esau upset his parents by marrying Judith and Basemath (see Gen. 26:34–35). Later, after the blessing had been stolen, when Esau "realized how displeasing the Canaanite women were to his father" (Gen. 28:8–9 NIV) he married another one, Mahalath.

So the child who does not (at least, openly) challenge his parents' authority comes to be cited as the example. "Look at Johnny; doesn't he look nice?" Or parents focus on behavior. "Your brother isn't crying . . ." "Why can't you be like . . . ?" The obedience of one child fuels the disobedience of another. But the problem is not confined to childhood or adolescence; the accusations plague us into adulthood.

2. Parents with unrealistic standards.

A growing number of young adults struggle to deal with their parents' standards. In many homes, standards were set (without consultation) or negotiation "for her own good," or "because I say so."

Parents themselves can create or encourage rebellious children. Many parents try to relive their lives through their child, or suffocate the freedom and integrity of the child, in an effort to be a good parent.

Steve's mother's hopes for a career as a classical pianist were ended when she became pregnant during her freshman year at a college conservatory. She attempted to live out her thwarted dreams by insisting that her only child be a pianist. However, the lessons, the practice, the battles of egos and wills produced, not a classical pianist, but a guy who plays with a jazz combo six nights a week.

Steve overcame his rebellion by forgiving his mother's "martial law" over his ambition. Others, however, abandon their talents completely or opt for ongoing skirmishes.

Some adults need to forgive their parent's sexual standards. One friend of mine has sexual and religious hang-ups engendered by a mother who "hated" her body and femininity and by a father who looked elsewhere for love and affection.

The mother shrieks in horror at the openness and honesty (gained after extensive counseling) which characterize her daughter's home . . . and blushes at the bluntness of her grandchildren's conversations. The risk is that the daughter may go overboard to compensate for her own scars, making her children the object of two wills.

Other parents manipulate their children, even after marriage. The Word states, "For this reason, a man will leave his father and mother and become united to his wife" (Gen. 2:24 NIV), a position Jesus restated in Matthew 19:5.

Because a lot of marriages have been destroyed or hamstrung by meddling in-laws, some must forgive their parental control over the choice of a marriage partner. In many cases, when parents have refused to accept their child's choice, the couple married out of defiance. Years later, the son/daughter recognized the wisdom of the parental reservations, but stuck it out in martyr marriages "for better or worse." But some parents cannot resist the "I-told-you-so" commentaries.

And a few parents refuse to admit that their objections have proved unfounded. Though their child has made a good marriage, they continue their criticisms of the mate. Forgiving this ongoing problem is perhaps harder than forgiving a parent who has been proven correct in his criticism.

3. Parents with the BIG ME/little you syndrome

Many children have had to deal with suppressed anger reflected in BIG ME (and, therefore, always right parent) versus little you (what would you know?) relationships. Some children spend a lifetime trying to win their parents' confidence. This BIG ME/little you relationship is amplified by the presence of a superachiever brother or sister to whom they assume they are always being compared.

As part of this BIG ME/little you syndrome, despite a child's sincere denials, the parent may demand: "Don't lie to me." Then, when the truth has exonerated the child, the parent seeks no forgiveness. And another notch is made in the child's belt of unforgiveness.

Many parents, ill-equipped for and threatened by parenting, attempt to preserve their authority by refusing to allow verbal challenges. Children are not allowed to sass; whiners are sent to their rooms. "I don't want to hear *another word*" ends too many conversations and confrontations and produces too many scars.

4. Parents who divorce

Children from homes broken by divorce have a set

of unique problems. And so do their parents. We must understand *those* problems before we can attempt to forgive those parents.

A parent must be more than biological or financial; abundance does not consist of the "loot" provided for the offspring. The post-war model of father as economic producer is counter-productive to the agenda of Christian parenting.

Some parents resent offspring who forced marriage before emotional readiness. So some teens become adult-mate-parent, in rapid succession. Their legal and symbolic adulthood became a fact long before the emotional. Some children eventually learn of the smoldering resentment toward them: "If it weren't for you, I'd be . . ."

That's one reason we're seeing an escalation of divorce among couples married twenty to twenty-five years. They did not believe they could choose *not* to marry. But after years of resentment, now that the children are grown and on their own, divorce seems the answer, especially for men struggling with the mid-life crisis.

With the rise in the divorce rate, a growing number of children must forgive parents who have divorced. Unfortunately some parents try a game of one-upmanship that escalates until there is a winner—no matter how many years it takes. And children skillfully learn to play one parent against the other.

Needless to say, more are injured by the fallout than by the explosion. The issues become more complicated when one or both remarry.

Parents sometimes mellow across the years, and want forgiveness for the years of assorted pain and tension. You may be put into the crisis by being somewhat reluctant to grant it.

Perhaps your parents divorced;
    perhaps you were fought over or manipulated;
       perhaps there is still an occasional flareup.
After all, old wounds still hurt on cold days.

But you can make the decision to forgive; if not the whole, the parts. Some will take longer; some will be delayed by individuals who insist on revenge and justice or having "my say." But it's your decision.

5. *The absentee parents*

Some parents simply never are around.

Some of us have grown up with a tradition of parents who are absent because of work obligations. Many seem to think the chief criterion of successful parenting is the economics of the family life style. "Just look at what I provide . . ."

In a consumer age, many parents *measure* their effectiveness by the things they give their children. We pride ourselves on "quality" time rather than quantity. Dr. James Dobson rejects this as a guilt-reducing cop-out. I would go a step further to suggest it as an easily-memorized anesthetic for troubled consciences. God's design includes *two* active parents in a child's life.

After all, a man's life is more than his abundance of possessions. A father's legacy consists of more than an estate to be left to his children (or to be fought over). Somehow courageous parents must risk saying no to material luxuries, in order to say yes to emotional and spiritual needs.

And, in an equally courageous step, some children must decide to forgive absentee parents.

6. *The deceased parent*

There are parents who still haunt or taunt from their graves. You can't go to a dead parent to voice your forgiveness, but the burden can be ended.

Consider "adopting a parent." Thousands of

lonely senior citizens in nursing homes and housing complexes designed for the elderly have been forgotten. I'm not suggesting penance but an effort to make another's life more meaningful. Directors of nursing centers can supply names of people who receive no mail, who are never visited, who wait alone to die in the warehouses we've built to "store" them.

If you don't want to become personally involved, some anonymous gestures would also be welcome..

To be able to forgive we must:

1. *Admit the need exists.* Denial only makes the task more difficult to face. Spend some time releasing the memories. Like a visit to a dentist, the drilling is uncomfortable, but the end result is beneficial.

2. *Risk the confrontation.* Once you have admitted your feelings and inventoried the situation, you may have to risk confronting an uncommunicative parent who does not want to remember. But you will never know until you take the risk.

3. *Talk . . . share . . . listen.* It may require more than one session. Let the parent know you're bringing up the subject not to induce pain but to seek relief from the pressure.

You can make a decision to forgive your parents—if not everything, then one part at a time.

Chronic rehashing and rearranging of old thoughts serve only to *avoid* the real issues. But you may have to ignore another recital of wrongs. The words of Paul are still good advice! "(Love) keeps no record of wrongs" (1 Cor. 13:5 NIV).

There are canyons in our hearts in which the air is stale and through which the Spirit would blow fresh winds if we allow. But it will be too late in some cases. Delaying only intensifies the burden to be lifted.

Holding a grudge or nursing a resentment against

a parent or stroking the scars while trying to be super parent to *your* children is enormously energy-draining.

And if the parent doesn't change, your responsibility to forgive *as an adult* is not negated.

If you choose not to forgive
you forever remain a child.
Forgiveness is a decision.

Forgiving:
Children

"Get out! I've had it! I've taken all I can stand! Gary, get your stuff and get out of here, *now!*"

A few years ago, the idea that this command could be voiced would have frightened John, a forty-seven-year-old executive. But after all that had transpired in these last several months, the conversation seemed predestined, inevitable.

Gary looked at his father and merely shrugged his shoulders. John turned and walked out of his son's room, down the hall, and into his own bedroom, to fall across his bed, weeping hysterically.

A few minutes later he heard the slam of the door, the squeal of tires as his son backed his car out of the driveway. Suddenly the house was quiet.

As he lay in the darkness, he remembered the first time he had seen that tiny boy in the

97

hospital nursery. He remembered the Easter Sunday when the baby had been dedicated to the Lord.

John had prided himself on the fact that he had not merely biologically fathered the child and then left the rearing to the mother. His decision not to be an absentee father like some of his colleagues had made an impact on his salary and bank balance, but it had been worth it—or so he had thought.

Now . . . he wondered. *Where have I gone wrong? What could I have done differently?*

For over a year he had gone to his office wearing the haggard look of a man who had put in hours in bed, without sleeping. How many nights had he lain awake, waiting to hear a car in the driveway and the slam of the back door that indicated his son was home for what was left of the night? How many loud angry confrontations had there been?

Every pronouncement of the successes of his neighbor's son rings in John's ears as a denouncement of himself and his son. That fear is in the heart of every parent of a child who "doesn't make it," although we may try to hide it. "Train up a child in the way he should go: and when he is old, he will not depart from it" (Prov. 22:6). Amen? Amen!

Besides, how could or how dare a parent go wrong with all the resources available? Surely PTA, Parent Effectiveness Training, encounter groups, James Dobson, Tim LaHaye, Charlie Shedd, books, magazines, experts, and cassettes could make a difference!

But there are silent Father's Days and hushed Mother's Days—when the cards do not come and the phone does not ring.

John remembers the times he had gotten up the middle of the night to chase away the bad dreams of a little boy. How many times had he opened his wallet to his son's wants? Where had he gone wrong? How did independence become hostility, then rebellion, then open warfare?

How many fathers' successes had he coveted? How many times had he watched the other kids on the block—kids who seemed to make it to adulthood with a minimum of wear and tear on their parents.

Perhaps he was to blame. Perhaps if he had not pushed the hair issue so strongly; perhaps if . . .

But it is too late to reparent this twenty-three-year-old. Gary is an adult and it is time to let him live with the adult consequences of his choices.

Thou shalt not covet thy neighbor's son or daughter! Wouldn't that make an interesting commandment today?

Weary of requesting prayer for their son or daughter, and fearing that someone in the congregation knows their troubles, many parents fill our church pews week after week. They covet missed opportunities for their children, who are on drugs, or unable to hold a job, or rebellious.

And some evangelical parents just don't like their kids.

You've given your all—worked two jobs and done without so that they could have the best—yet they want more.

Years ago I had a friend who charged a couple of hundred dollars' worth of clothes at a men's shop in his hometown. His father discovered, when checking on the bill, that his son had purchased, among other "necessary" items, a forty-dollar belt. The father had paid only $4.95 for his own belt.

Via an expensive long-distance phone call, he made sure that his son understood that he could use the belt for something other than holding up his pants!

Why do hostilities develop between father and

son, mother and daughter? How do children learn to skillfully play one parent against the other? How do they learn to manipulate effectively and smoothly? Too often, because father manipulates mother, or vice versa.

How many mothers give their whole lives to their children—vetoing their own rights and luxuries as a person? Many parents secretly (but still guiltily) think, *I wish I could be as good to myself as I am to my kids.* But they also say, "I don't know what I'd do if I didn't have my kids—they're all I've got."

Some divorced parents are captured by the notion, *I failed as a spouse, so I'll be a superparent.* In the last generation an unhealthy trend has developed for parents to live for their kids. But the kids eventually leave home and the nest is empty. Discovering they have built a "one-flesh" relationship with their children rather than with their mate sends many middle-aged couples to the divorce courts.

In my work, I listen to single mothers who feel trapped by their kids; who are weary of playing a role, of being both mother and father. They envy the freedom of the childless single and think, *If only I didn't have kids . . .*

I recently counseled a young woman who hates her child because he physically resembles his father. The woman had not wanted to marry the man but felt obligated to do so when she found herself pregnant. All her dreams and ambitions were swept away. Now the child suffers because of the mother's unresolved conflicts. Such "bottled-up" feelings fuel child abuse.

Churches which have organized "Mother's Day Out" programs are of great help to parents who have run out of resources, thereby becoming prime candidates for child-abusers.

Some parents need to forgive their child because

the child has failed or has rejected the expectations they have held for the child.

Some of the Little League shenanigans I see around the country demonstrate the fact that many dads are living out their dreams of athletic success through their sons and are pushing little bodies far beyond their physiological endurance and capacity. There are just as many baseball moms who would just as soon deck the umpire if he makes a call contrary to their opinion. Hell hath no fury like an irritated Little League parent; some of them seem to leave their parental love in the parking lot.

And what about the parents who discover their child is not merely defiant or rebellious, but gay? That painful reality cannot permanently be ignored.

The son of a minister friend came "out of the closet," much to the humiliation of his parents. When the son announced his sexual preference at high school graduation, the father declared his son dead. Ten years later, the son is a prominent professional— without one penny of assistance or one word of encouragement from his dad. Occasionally the mother spends some time with her son, but the father never mentions his name.

The father has had to continually reinforce all the barriers because the Lord has provided so many opportunities to break them down: Father's Day, Christmas, his own birthday, his son and namesake's birthday.

Some parents remain silent or inwardly cringe with some statements about "fags," "fruits," or "queers." Unfortunately some parents help convince their children that they are homosexually oriented when they read the riot act after comparatively innocent adolescent same-sex experimentation. Others have refused to answer questions on the subject or have not provided a climate in which those questions could be faced.

Tragically a lot of parents are unable to say, "I'm sorry," or to initiate the forgiveness process. Some have punished children—demanding their silence, an end to their professions of innocence. "We know you're guilty," only to discover later that he was telling the truth!

That is why the story of the seeking father still profoundly affects us 2000 years after Jesus first told it. We can identify with the struggle of the two boys and their father.

We like the sentimental aspects of the prodigal son story. But what went through the mind of the father each day as he wandered down to the gate to wait—to stare far down the road until darkness fell? What sent him back, night after night, aware that his other son protested his vigil? What did he think as he blew out the lamp and tried to fall asleep?

The passage in Luke 15 has some interesting points. The fact of decision is clearly reported, "When he came to his senses . . . he got up and went to his father" (15:17, 20 NIV).

But the father also made some decisions. "While he was still a long way off, his father saw him and was filled with compassion for him" (v. 20). The father did not wait until the son had reached the gate. Parents often fail to thank the Lord for the first signs of a *breakthrough!* This father recognized his son's good intensions as a *sign!* "He was still a long way off," but he was coming home!

We need to recall one fact: the father went out daily to wait for his son at the gate. I personally wish he had gone down to the pig pen—but Jesus let him go only halfway. Sometimes the wronged party has to initiate the recovery process, to reestablish the ties, to heal the wounds.

The second decision the father made was *to run* to meet the son. He could have waited, arms crossed, an icy stare reflecting his displeasure. (I remember an occasion or two when my dad didn't say a word—but I was paralyzed by his gaze.) This father was so eager to see his son, he wasn't concerned about "saving face." His body language gave him away.

As the son begins his carefully rehearsed speech, his father interrupts his story: "Quick! Bring the *best* robe ... put a ring on his finger ..." and then he orders, "And bring the *fattened* calf!" Somehow we have overlooked the fact that the father had so anticipated this day that he had already been feeding that calf. Every time he walked to the feed lot—that calf rekindled his hope that his son would return.

Thirdly, "he threw his arms around him and kissed him." This kid, reeking with the stench of hog pens, could not have been especially appealing to anyone but a parent.

But we also note that the father imposed no waiting period to test his son's remorse. Forgiveness was not doled out stingily—it was complete and immediate.

There are too many strained relationships in too many evangelical families. Sometimes funerals or near-tragedies reunite families who have become hardly more than strangers. But too often reunions are merely "cease-fires," with the hostilities later resumed.

A lot of "kids" in exile would like to come home, but their parents have demanded an "unconditional surrender." The price for return is so high that no child could return and retain a shred of dignity.

I spent this morning, a day off from a busy schedule, not writing as I had planned, but playing with three small boys. Last night I carried one of them in from the car, sound asleep, and put him into bed. For a long time afterward, I stood in the darkness thinking, *I would have been a good father.*

That was the first time that had ever happened and I wondered briefly why it hadn't happened before.

Today the little guy awoke, asking, "Where my friend is?" Interesting grammar—I'm his friend, nameless for that moment, but still his friend. Perhaps if his mother repeatedly drills my name, he will catch on before I leave.

Today I fixed his swingset and let him "help" me, although I could have finished the project in half the time by myself.

But my writer's guilt appeared to condemn me: "Jason Towner, you should have been writing during that time. You have a deadline to meet!" Then I remembered how important my swingset and toys had been when I was that age. How many times had I requested repairs and been told "When I get to it"?

That rusty old swingset purchased at a garage sale is important in Chip Killingsworth's world—as essential as an electric typewriter in my world. I need to remember that Chip needs that to become all that he can become.

I can't blame his dad because he is busy. Yet I am tempted to put the guilt-trip on the father, teasing him gently: "What is more important today than your child's swingset?"

See, rusty swingsets are more than they seem. They become forts and airplanes and spaceships and memory-makers in the creative world of children. Such games allow children to experience fantasy within the safety of reality. It is as important for a four-year-old to swing enthusiastically and demand, "Hey, look at me . . ." as it is for me to share my latest publication success.

What about the older adult child? All kinds of crazy things—sometimes small, forgotten, or insignificant by one set of standards—stain, scratch, and blemish the delicate ties between parent and child. Angry adults punish their parents by limiting the amount of time spent with them, or by warehousing them. The ultimate segregation is to put senior citizens "with their own kind" where we assume (and repeatedly reassure ourselves) they will feel more "at home."

And these discarded parents ask, "Wonder why they don't come around anymore?" or "They're too busy for me now that I am old. . . . What if I had been too busy for them when they were young?"

Forgiving your child who is now an adult is a tough task (particularly for acts committed as a child), and there is no guarantee the child won't break your heart or disappoint you again. That's the risk the parent as forgiver must take.

Forgiving:
Life

How old were you when you first heard, "That's life?" or "It rains on the just and the unjust" or "Who said life was supposed to be fair?"

But that doesn't make it any easier when you are confronted with the fact that:

—your next-door neighbor inherited a lot of money
—other people have healthier bodies
bigger homes
nicer furniture
better-behaved children
mates who really love them
—you're getting older
—the boss's son got the job you were promised
—some people can eat hot fudge sundaes and never gain a pound

—X doesn't tithe and still prospers.

And some of us may ask, "Why does it have to happen to me?"

All of us must go through that season of the night, when God seems far from us. There are times we are asked to sing the Lord's song in a strange land, when faith is nourished by struggle.

When you were a child, did you ever want to ride the horse or the stagecoach or the elephant or the spaceship outside the grocery store? Sometimes your parents inserted the dime, but nothing happened, despite your loud protests.

And sometimes someone had already discovered, and a sign proclaimed, that the machine was "out of order." Did you ever refuse to accept that fact? How could the horse be "out of order"?

However, there were those times when your mom or dad didn't furnish the necessary dime. Perhaps you had been bad, and you were not going to get to ride the horse. Did you ever throw a temper tantrum to get your ride?

How do you explain the unexplainable?

Dr. Robert Merckel from Crystal Cathedral Ministries has concluded that a lot of *adults* are into a vending-machine theology and psychology:

1. Insert money
2. Make selection
3. Expect results.

I've dropped a lot of coins into candy machines, expecting a little sugary treat as a reward for a long, hard day's work. Through the glass panel I could see what the machine had to offer. So I made my decision, selected the corresponding number, dropped in the coins, pressed the panel, and watched my Zonkers or Snickers or cheese and crackers drop. I opened the hatch, picked up my snack and off I went—no conversation, no personal contact.

But occasionally, when I put in my money—nothing happens. Now, just between you and me, what do you do?

—Say: "Oh, well. I didn't really need the calories."

—Talk to the machine: "Hey, what do you mean taking my quarter?"

—Shake the machine?

—Bang the coin return repeatedly?

—Put in another quarter and cross your fingers?

—All of the above.

Life itself can be like that candy machine. Sometimes things don't seem to work out, despite the scriptural promise: "All things work together for good . . ." (Rom. 8:28).

Sometimes I simply do not understand life. My mind may be too limited or underdeveloped to handle physics, chemistry, or botany. Sometimes I don't know enough to ask the right questions (and because I have an ego to defend, I'm not about to ask a stupid question). And sometimes the answer is so complex that I just "tune it out."

But I have mortar in the cracks of my faith to keep the walls up. That mortar is the awareness about which Isaiah wrote: "Fear not, for I have redeemed you; I have called you by name; you are mine" (Isa. 43:2 NIV).

He knows your name too. God loves you and is committed to you. I firmly believe that verse of Scripture that I have written on the flyleaf of so many books: "For I know the plans I have for you," declares the Lord, "plans to prosper you and not to harm you, plans to give _____ (insert your name) a hope and a future" (Jer. 29:11 NIV).

Why didn't Jeremiah just use one word, either *future* or *hope?* Why did he need both? Because the clocks of eternity are not set by earthly standards of time; He is there!

On earth, each of us has 365 days in a year and twenty-four hours in a day. Everyone gets sixty seconds in a minute and sixty minutes in an hour, whether a Zulu warrior or a Kansas farmhand. Yet, some of us seem to get more done in any time segment than others.

Life makes no promises that, even if we follow what we believe to be its rules, we will always succeed.

Do you ever watch "All-Star Wrestling"? I've concluded that that program, to a greater degree than other programs which compete for the viewing audience, is symbolic of life itself.

In "All-Star Wrestling," the viewer recognizes a good guy and a bad guy. Generally we know the outcome of the match before the referee explains the rules and the opening bell rings. The good guy is probably going to lose unless a miracle happens.

The good guy is a clean-cut, all-American kid. Old ladies cheer for him because he is like a grandson to them. He often gets the stuffing beaten out of him because he is too naïve. Despite the fans' loud warning to "stay out of the opponent's corner," he never seems to hear. He charges in where angels fear to tread.

The bad guy sneers and snarls while the crowd (which is obviously prejudiced) boos and scowls. He arrogantly prophesies what he will do to the good guy: "I'll tear your head off . . ."

Often, when it looks as if the good guy has breathed his last, somehow he summons the strength to get one shoulder off the mat before the referee's "One! Two! Three!" So the match continues. Sometimes the good guy "has" to break the rules. Then the bad guy complains to the ref and the crowd protests loudly.

Not infrequently a favorite tactic is hair-pulling, which, of course, the ref never sees. So he asks the bad guy, "Did you pull his hair?"

And he always responds with an innocent air, as though he is offended that the ref would even ask!

When the good guy has simply taken all he can stand, his temper wears thin, and he becomes serious. He has the bad guy on the run and pleading, but, somehow, the good guy is caught off-guard for a split second, and the bad guy kicks the good guy in the stomach and takes control again.

Doesn't that resemble life itself? Haven't you wanted to just lie there and hear the ref count you out? Haven't you wanted to give up and ask, "Which way to the showers?"

I think there are three kinds of people in this world:

whiners—who whine about the "unfairness" of life.

wonderers—who become the philosophers of life.

winners—who make lemonade out of the lemons of life.

Some of us are crisis-oriented, bouncing from one crisis to another, needing a cause or a predicament to survive. Some carry placards or march or protest or sign petitions or write their congressman about whatever it is that is upsetting them at that particular moment. Some of us wait for God to act or intervene or to set the matter straight.

There are a lot of things in life that I cannot explain:

polio

multiple sclerosis

cancer

cerebral palsy

Down's syndrome

car wrecks caused by drunken drivers

airplane crashes
explosions
child abuse
wife-beating
the premature death of a good man
crib death
rape
robbery
house fires
floods
famines
pestilence
tornadoes
hurricanes

Most of us have entertained the thought that the government should spend as much money on disease research as has been spent on sending men to the moon. But, perversely, some people are happy only when they are ill, impressing others with specialists, and diseases, and the scientific names of wonder drugs.

Much of our illness is pychosomatic—a crying out for affirmation, for attention. For some, illness becomes a respectable suicide.

Who can explain life? I can't.

But I do know there are twenty-four hours in a day; sixty minutes in an hour; sixty seconds in a minute; and that each of us has the same measure of time!

In my impatience there have been those times when I have echoed Mary and Martha's bitter words to Jesus: "Lord, *if* you had been here, our brother would not have died" (John 11:32). In other words, "Where have you been?"

Not everyone was healed by Jesus. We have the mistaken notion that he healed everyone within a half-mile radius.

Jesus' life proves there are some paradoxes, some ironies, some unbelievables that *do* happen.

So we have to forgive life. That, too, is a decision.

Forgiving:
Those Out to Get Me

I am afraid!

I am afraid . . . that if you walked through the corridors of my life and found some of the hidden passageways . . . you would reject me!

One of the greatest challenges of Christianity has been its adherents' inability to trust and forgive each other. Every Christian has had those moments lying in the dark considering the possibilities. *What if ——— finds out about ———? What will I say? What will I do?*

So I won't tell you everything. Why should I?

You're keeping your secrets from me. In most relationships, there is a carefully balanced set of scales with equal portions of revelations. We strive to tip the scales in our favor by diverting attention to others. To do this, sometimes we throw the listener a little nugget like:

"If you knew what I know about him . . ."

"How did you find out about . . . ?"

"Promise you won't tell a soul!"

"If one word of this gets out . . ."

"You won't believe this, but . . ."

And then we retreat self-righteously: "I'd better not say any more." (A hint can be as damaging as an entire accusation, because the listener surmises something more titillating than the truth.)

People respond: "Oh, you know me . . . I'm not going to tell."

Some of us crave gossip intensely. We have to know! We will not rest until we know!

"Tell me!"

"Tell me!"

"TELL ME!"

I'll tell you—if you tell me your secrets *first!* Well, what are you waiting for?

Actually my confession could be quite harmless by your standards—as yours could be by mine. But we all suspect that the district attorney or the CIA or the FBI is vaguely interested.

What haunts you today? What really bothers you? I'm not talking about unconfessed sin or unforgiven sin—but *unforgotten sin*. We are the wardens of our own prisons of guilt; Satan is merely a periodic visitor.

In my work, I hear a lot of things I wish I hadn't. I know a lot of things I wish I didn't.

The other day I was astounded by a friend's report that another friend is a homosexual. He "has it from a good source." How reliable is the source considering the impact of the disclosure? And what was his motive in telling me? That rumor with its implications has become another of my burdens.

Such experiences ("Can you believe it?"—and

too often, we can) influence our own lives. The fear of inadequate or conditional forgiveness keeps a lot of people from seeking the help they need. Premature or indiscriminate confession comes back to haunt us.

And what about teasing? Are those who tease us really "out to get us?"

Why do people tease? Sometimes it's because they themselves feel threatened. Teasing constantly reminds those who are teased of *their* inadequacies—they are never what they should be. Some of us will *never* eliminate the scars made by teasing which focused on an aspect of our anatomy or personality.

Our immediate temptation is to retaliate, to return the volley, to wound the wounder. All of us have parameters within which we *permit* or *tolerate* teasing. Yet anger fueled by a teasing remark may cause us to strike quickly with a verbal jab to stun the teaser.

Brooding over "what I should have said" can be dangerous because it keeps the incident fresh. Retorting spontaneously serves as a warning shot: "Hey, two can play this game!"

You cannot get ahead of a good teaser. Don Rickles is a millionaire because he can bounce back, seemingly without thinking. Audiences love to see him get someone "good."

But not all teasers are humorous or verbal; some are cruel, some are silent.

"Oh, but *I wouldn't tease you if I didn't like you.*" Poor logic! Am I supposed to squirm in discomfort because you "like" me?

I have a friend who teases me about celibacy, offering me "practical" hints on sublimation. So, one day when he was being especially obnoxious, I asked: "How would *you* deal with your sexuality if *your* wife left you? You've teased me and offered these tacky suggestions—which one would work for you?"

He tried to retreat but I pursued him tenaciously until he cried uncle. As we talked through the problem, I was able to share some of my feelings. Because of his teasing and my confrontation, he gained a glimpse of understanding of my single life.

Teasing might be more fun if it weren't so bloody, so scary, so threatening. But it is easier for us to say glibly, "I'm sorry" or to appeal to the old "kiss-and-make-up" routine than to eliminate the skill from our verbal repertoires.

I think Jesus has a sense of humor—but He never teases! He laughs *with* us, not at us! It's fantastic to know that the One who knows us best, who knows every vulnerability, every weakness and could use it to His advantage . . . doesn't.

One reason I'm writing on forgiveness is that I am still struggling with the whole process, still trying to understand what forgiveness means. Will I ever get beyond the apprenticeship? I desperately hunger for forgiveness. Perhaps I'm trying to understand the process before I enjoy the promise. It may be that the pieces will fit together only in eternity's dawn.

The burden is often complicated by those who will not accompany us on the forgiveness journey. Some people may be willing to forgive, but *only* on their timetable and their terms. Many demand an unconditional surrender in their personal conflicts—a surrender which does not demand our involvement in rebuilding the defeated.

Their forgiveness demands that you'll never think of doing it again. "He'll think twice before he tries that again!" they mutter between clenched teeth. And some people are sorrier that they got caught than for the offense itself.

Recently because of the violent mud-slinging personality clash between two politicians in an election campaign, one candidate declared to enthusiastic supporters, "I don't want to *just* win. I want to give my opponent the political beating of his career! I want him out of politics ... for good! I want to see him humiliated at the polls in November!" His supporters roared!

And he won, two to one. The opponent retired from politics. But the final chapter of the victor's political biography has yet to be written.

Conversely the United States chose, after World War II, not to sow salt in the fields of Japan and Germany, but to invest in their economies. They lost the war militarily but won economically. Enemies have become allies and financial partners and eventually stiff competitors—and American homes are full of items produced by those two nations.

In the Old Testament is the account of Shimei, a clansman of Saul, throwing rocks at David and his entourage as they fled in humiliation from Absalom.

A soldier named Abishai demanded of David, "Why should this dead dog curse my lord the king? Let me go over and cut off his head" (2 Sam. 16:9 NIV). How easy it is to become involved in other people's battles.

David responded, "Leave him alone ... It may be that the Lord will see my distress and repay me with good for the cursing I am receiving today" (2 Sam. 16:13, NIV).

Later, after Absalom was defeated, Shimei approached David to make amends for his tacky behavior. "Do not remember," he pleaded, "how your servant did wrong on the day my lord the king left Jerusalem. May the king put it out of mind" (2 Sam. 19:19 NIV). In other words, Forget it! Abishai, always loyal to the king and itching to be royal executioner, replied, "Shouldn't Shimei be put to death for this? He cursed the Lord's anointed!" (19:21 NIV). There will always be someone quoting the law, offering us "shoulds."

The king graciously spared Shimei and sealed the promise with an oath. However, years later, as David lay dying, a different attitude prevailed. He shared with Solomon the various secrets of successful kingship (see 1 Kings 2:2–9). Then he mentioned Shimei.

> "And remember, you have with you Shimei son of Gera, the Benjamite from Bahurim, who called down bitter curses on me the day I went to Mahanaim. When he came down to meet me at the Jordan, I swore to him by the Lord: 'I will not put you to death by the sword.' But now, *do not consider him innocent. You are a man of wisdom; you will know what to do to him. Bring his gray head down to the grave in blood.*"
>
> (1 Kings 2:8–9 NIV, *italics mine*)

The only thing lacking was an exclamation mark. Perhaps David was too exhausted to punctuate that comment. The next verse reads, "David rested with his fathers" (1 Kings 2:10 NIV). He died cursing his enemy.

Couldn't David have taken those words to the grave? Wouldn't it have been better for Solomon to have begun his reign without a deathbed request for revenge? Yet how could he ignore his father's last request?

Eventually after disposing of a few other matters of state, Solomon called for Shimei to show him who was boss. He allowed Shimei to build a new house but forbade him to travel. "the day you leave and cross the Kidron Valley, *you can be sure you will die;* your blood will be on your own head" (1 Kings 2:37 NIV, *italics mine*).

Three years passed before two of Shimei's slaves fled to Gath. Shimei naturally pursued them, and (coincidentally!) Solomon was informed. Perhaps someone close to Solomon had it in for Shimei. Or perhaps the slaves were encouraged to flee to force Shimei to violate Solomon's command.

So, Shimei died and "The kingdom was now firmly established in Solomon's hands" (1 Kings 2:46 NIV). He began his reign settling in blood his father's unfinished business.

I wish David, a recipient of such enormous forgiveness, could have granted forgiveness as he crossed worlds. But he didn't!

What unfinished business—battles, prejudices, missed opportunities—have you passed on to your children? It's not only the Hatfields and the McCoys who pass unforgiveness from generation to generation.

What have you shared with your friends? Have you drawn mutual aggression treaties which have involved other people in your feuds and battles and skirmishes? What fuels your feuds? Is your problem too caustic for the salve of forgiveness?

The first task in forgiving those "out to get you" is disarming the arsenals.

We store a lot of weapons "just in case" we're attacked. Most of us anxiously seek the new ultimate weapon to give us the super advantage over our opponent, whether it be

a wife
a child
a business colleague or competitor
a neighbor.

That's why we listen to gossip. Tidbits of gossip become warheads to detonate the heavier ammunition in our arsenals.

During World War II, in the Pacific and Atlantic,

mines packed with explosives floated under the surface of the shipping lanes. A ship, plowing through the water, could detonate the mine, ripping open the hull of the ship and sending cargo and men to the bottom.

Remember all those World War II movies on TV every afternoon after school? The captain would call for the periscope, sight the Japanese destroyer, and order the torpedoes readied. Then came the moment of intense drama as he stood, sensing death and victory, realizing that by his command a ship could go down to a watery grave. The adrenalin raced through his veins (and through ours as we munched on our after-school-but-don't-eat-enough-to-spoil-your-dinner snacks). Then we heard his command: *"Fire!"*

There are a lot of verbal mines and torpedoes in our lives, just waiting to be detonated. We know the techniques for launching the weapons in our stockpiles; we have drilled in preparation for the opportunity.

Occasionally the crew of the enemy ship escaped —never knowing how close they had come to disaster. Often we, too, are unaware of how close we come to a devastating attack.

So we need a process to disarm the arsenals, to reduce the kill-power. In essence, we need a Strategic Arms Limitation Treaty (SALT) for our emotions. That's why some friends are really enemies, their arsenals loaded to capacity with all the garbage they know.

What's in your inventory of weapons, armed and ready for launching at a moment's notice? Perhaps you have prided yourself in saying you will not "strike first," that you store only defense weapons.

Wouldn't it be neat if we could have one afternoon a week when we could talk about what we're really thinking about, say every Tuesday, from 12:00–4:00 P.M.? You could feel free to say:

"I think my wife is having an affair . . ." .

"My husband doesn't love me anymore . . ."

"I'm about to lose my job . . ."

"I think my daughter is sleeping with her boy-friend . . ."

"My son is gay . . ."

"I'm afraid of you."

But it wouldn't work—honesty leads to vulnerability. That data would be at another's disposal the other 166 hours of the week. We would have to devise calculated formulas to control the information, to keep it "in hand." Sidney Jourard explains that "when you permit yourself to be known, you expose yourself not only to a lover's balms, but also to a hater's bombs! When he knows you, he knows just where to plant them for maximum effect."

We understand that all too well!

What can encourage me to open up my arsenals to reveal all my weapons? If I show my vulnerability, you'll know where to attack. And I would have to give up

cynicism

sarcasm

ridicule

tongue-lashing.

So it becomes a question of decision-making. I don't want my opponents to take advantage of my spirituality or naïvete. Jesus mentions turning the other cheek—but does that work today?

I've thought about it and here is my conclusion. I would be willing to disarm my arsenal . . .

if you will disarm yours and

if you will disarm it *first!*

It's not that I don't trust you. I do, but you would encourage me a great deal if you would go first.

"No way!" you respond. You are as afraid as I to take the risk.

Then I must take the initiative and even if you do not reciprocate, I will gain by disarming. The burden of unforgiveness wreaks most havoc on the unforgiving.

One lady angrily demanded, "Are you saying I have to forgive my ex *before* he asks my forgiveness?"

I replied, "Yes, even if he *never* asks for your forgiveness." That was difficult for her to accept.

We're tempted to fantasize about that Big Moment when someone asks our forgiveness. So, while showering or waiting in line to cash a check, or while the dentist works on a cavity, we act as playwrights carefully staging it in the theater of our minds. Most of the time, *we* have the best lines.

Forgiveness sometimes is the only way adults can abandon childish behavior and self-persecution routines. Forgiveness requires a decision. Are you willing to disarm your arsenals *without* a written guarantee that "those out to get you" will follow suit?

Could it be that your "opponent" is as anxious for forgiveness as you are and your forgiveness will open the door for him to forgive and receive the blessing of forgiveness?

There is an Eastern legend about an elephant who was nearly shot by a hunter. Instead of defending himself aggressively, the elephant ran, pausing only momentarily—the slightest noise sending him thundering away again.

For weeks the elephant ran—motivated by fear and unaware that the big game hunter had died of a heart attack ten minutes after he fired at the animal.

Some of us have "elephant days" too. We shy away from issues that are no longer viable, run because of fears that have no basis, exhaust ourselves running.

These issues, these fears, these enemies waste our valuable life-time—time that could be spent basking in the bright sunshine of forgiveness, instead of cowering in the dark shadows of unforgiveness.

Forgiving:
The Bubble-bursters

All of us have dreams and ambitions—bubbles to chase. But for every bubble-chaser, there is a bubble-burster, a dream-popper, waiting to destroy our dreams. Some of us need to forgive those who dash our hopes. Bubble-chasers thrive on goals. Generally they design new goals before reaching the old ones.

Superachievers write books and give lectures and spend much time in airports going "to and fro" spreading the word about attaining success. And those bubble-chasers are the ones who buy the books and tapes and go to hear them speak.

Recently, 10,000 people paid a good fee to hear a group of "success superstars" reveal their secrets. But God has never called anyone to be successful; only obedient.

Most of us have had bubbles burst and have had to peel

the gum off our faces. Some of us never try again, embalming our dreams; others find the collapse a relief from the pressure. Many are drained of creativity.

My friend Susan ate, slept, and lived premed— and fell in love with a fellow student, probably because they spent so much time together in labs. When Susan realized her competitiveness with John was a barrier to her equally important goal of marriage, she changed her major to science education and got a teaching degree. John dug deeper into his books. After graduation, they married. A lot of her friends envied her because they thought she would be on easy street financially.

However, because of the rigorous time demands of med school, they drifted apart. The day John received his M.D., he had divorce papers served on Susan. Susan's bubble (being a doctor's wife) burst. Feeling betrayed, she successfully sued—John must pay her 40 percent of his income for twenty years, even if she remarries. The judge ruled in her favor because she had worked to make *their* dream *his* reality.

Like me, many of my peers were first-generation college students whose parents never felt really comfortable on college campuses with "doctors" and "professors" everywhere. They took us to campus and stood under shade trees talking to other equally uneasy parents while we raced about "matriculating." But our parents were often willing to make sacrifices to give their sons and daughters an education of which to be proud.

As evangelicals sent their kids to colleges to become teachers a generation ago, so are those now-grown-up teachers sending *their* children to train for more sophisticated professions. Evangelical churches are proud of "their" kids who have now become professionals.

Mary and Bill married during their senior year in

college. Soon she became pregnant (not part of their plan) and Bill's med school bubble burst. He has spent the past ten years teaching biology in an inner-city high school. Bill blames Mary and, although he has accepted his "fate," he has not forgiven her. His grief is rekindled every time he reads of the accomplishments of the class of '65 in the alumni magazine—including those of his roommate, who became a physician.

Truthfully Bill's chances of making med school were doubtful—but his ego (and his parents') would never permit him to accept that. It is easier to believe Mary kept him from his dream. Tragically he has also resented the child.

Another bubbler had the opportunity to invest in "a sure thing, can't lose" oil well. He discussed the opportunity with his wife, a "practical" person who had never seen a rainbow, and was unwilling to dream. Frugal, cautious, "What about a rainy day?" she demanded. "Why gamble when our money is getting 5¾ percent interest day-in, day-out?" She talked him out of the investment and scolded him for his dreaming.

Like a hurt pup he retreated. He had so little self-confidence that he dared not take the risk.

The day, eight months later, when the well was a "gusher" and the investors (many of whom were friends) hit it "big," his marriage began its death dance. He curses himself daily for listening to his wife and has never let her forget her mistake.

Not all bubble-bursters are female. Men, too, find ways to destroy their wives' dreams.

The man who felt comfortable with a stay-at-home wife can't comprehend why she feels "unfulfilled." Or he feels threatened when she goes back to school. Or he limits her career to one in which her salary does not exceed his.

Some women marry bubble-chasers—ne'er-do-wells who couldn't "find themselves"—and have to live with a succession of burst bubbles. Parents have been embarrassed by sons who couldn't keep a job or "stay with it." Even high achievers make some family reunions tense and competitive. Others can relate stories of money "down the drain," and the "can't lose" deals that *did*.

Thousands wonder at college or high-school reunions: *What would have happened if I had married Tom instead of Steve?* Some mothers forever remind their daughters (and their sons-in-law) of the economic accomplishments of that someone "you could have married if you had listened to me."

The struggle to "make it" can be costly. Some attain their goal but find no peace, because new goals must be set. Some meet the goal(s) but lose their families, health, and sanity in the process. Others feel trapped because the psychological "pay-off" they coveted did not materialize or did not prove as exhilarating as they had expected.

The craving for success may be fueled by bad memories. Forgiveness seems foreign to one who has just read the latest best seller on success. We must forgive the dream-defeaters as well as those dreamers who are unable to live in the real world. We must forgive those we would like to blame for our defeat.

Have you listened closely to superachievers quoting Philippians 4:13? *"I* (in neon, please) can do *all things* through Christ which strengtheneth *me* (bright neon)." They offer the equivalent of a religious show-and-tell or "Let's Make a Deal." Sometimes we lose count of the number of *I's* or *me's* or *my's* used.

For the faithful, the verse should read, "I can do all things through *Christ* which strengtheneth me."

Some of us can't win because our goals are unrealistic; some will settle for second or third place; and some will remain on the sidelines, observing the success of others.

What about the "walking wounded" who wear defeat as a badge and refuse to try again? For those who have prematurely surrendered their dreams, their pain is deep and paralyzing, making them its prisoners. They expect no summons to renewal or tomorrow.

Sometimes only God can answer our "what if's":

What if X had happened instead of . . . ?

What if I had married _____ *instead of* _____?

What if that deal had gone through . . . ?

How can we put yesterday's burst bubbles in a forgiving context?

Lord, forgive my cowardice . . .

Lord, forgive my laziness . . .

Lord, forgive my failure to seize the opportunities You have brought into my life . . .

Lord, I did the best I could then—help me to accept the now of my life.

If we believe that Jesus is Lord of all, we must believe that He is also Lord of our burst bubbles. We need to examine our failures honestly and take our share of the blame. Excuses are out of place in the forgiveness process, even though analysis may uncover the fact that we ourselves are the main ingredient for our failure.

Many people work hard to accomplish goals and then throw them away on a whim; many try to keep proving something to someone. We need to accept the responsibility for sabotaging our own success.

God can give us victory over self-defeat; He can renew and strengthen and enable. But He awaits our invitation to work in our lives and dreams. He will not force us into spiritual *receivership!*

God likes learners. Whatever the circumstances, failure can be a learning experience. The ashes of yesterday fertilize the soil in which tomorrow's dreams grow.

Success often demands prepayment—long hours, warmed-over dinners, late nights, early mornings, noes that must be said.

All young couples dream—it's dangerous when they stop. Some of their dreams are unrealistic, but they're not written on tablets of stone.

But a lot of people give up their dreams for the dull routine of the Monday-Friday, nine-to-five shuffle. They know precisely what is demanded of them, what they can get by with. Many have the Thursday night prayer, *O Lord—one more day to go! If I can make it until tomorrow at three o'clock, I'm home free.* For them, work is so unimportant as to be boring.

Others love their work. They quote: "This is the day the Lord has made . . ." (Ps. 118:24 NIV), the day "to get with the program!" Each work day represents another opportunity to greet the morning and roll from bed, fresh, clear, all systems go.

Some of us work hard to follow the rainbow to its ever-elusive pot of gold. From early childhood we are intrigued by the beauty of a rainbow—the multi-colored expression of calm after the storm. But rainbows come *only after thunderstorms.* The more violent the storm, the brighter the rainbow.

Chasing rainbows can be serious, productive work. But some of us have discovered a question mark at rainbow's end. We ask, "Is this the best I can do?"

Occasionally life makes an unexpected turn, without a proper signal.

Old dreams can be replaced by new as part of the forgiveness process. Sometimes we find our goals change with the passage and the experience of the years. Our values change and, thus, our dreams. And forgiving one who has destroyed our dreams may open the way for a bigger, brighter future.

> And, it shall come to pass afterward, that I will pour out my spirit upon all flesh; and your sons and your daughters shall prophesy, your old men shall dream dreams, your young men visions. (Joel 2:28)

That covers us all: men, women, young, old. The reality: "I am making everything new!" (Rev. 21:5 NIV).

It takes a decision to forgive the bubble-bursters and to take a deep breath and dream again.

Forgiving:
The "I Can't Believe
It Happened to Me"

All of us face experiences that we would not choose. Someone does something to us or we suffer because of another's decision, made before all the possible consequences are considered.

All of us, saints or sinners, have skeletons in our closets. In some of our lives, unconfessed sin or misunderstood sin harrasses; in others, it is failure to meet an unattainable standard. We missed the mark—but did we ever *really* have a chance to hit it?

And all of us experience the "impossibles" of life. A young adult is killed in a freak accident; a child dies while being cared for by a friend. The unthinkable occurs today just as it did in history.

Tamar, the beautiful daughter of King David, realized that someday she would marry—and not just anyone. It would be a marriage which would strengthen the royal family. Her future seemed bright and promising.

However, her brother Amnon fell in love with her. Frustrated because of his infatuation, he eventually fell ill because "she was a virgin, and it seemed impossible for him to do anything to her" (2 Sam. 13:2 NIV), or apparently *about* her.

Amnon's friend Jonadab, who must have been somewhat like an ancient "Fonzie," finally asked him, "Why do you . . . look so haggard morning after morning?" (2 Sam. 13:4 NIV).

Amnon replied, "I'm in love with Tamar" (2 Sam. 13:4 NIV).

Instead of being shocked, Jonadab suggested to Amnon, "Go to bed and pretend to be ill . . . When your father comes to see you, say to him, 'I would like my sister Tamar to come and give me something to eat'" (2 Sam. 13:5 NIV).

Amnon followed his advice. When David came down to see his son, Amnon requested a special meal. David sent word to Tamar, "Go to the house of your brother Amnon and prepare some food for him" (2 Sam. 13:7 NIV).

Tamar went down to Amnon's house, merely following her father's instructions. She saw nothing unusual about the request; sick people tend to be finicky eaters. When the meal was prepared, Amnon refused to come into the dining room.

"'Send everyone out of here,' Amnon said. So everyone left him. Then Amnon said to Tamar, 'Bring the food here into my bedroom'" (2 Sam. 13:9–10 NIV). So Tamar took the bread to him.

Then he grabbed her. "Come to bed with me, my sister" (2 Sam. 13:11 NIV), he suggested lewdly. If she thought he was kidding, she quickly realized his intent.

"Don't, my brother!" (2 Sam. 12:12 NIV). As he

tightened his grip, she continued, "Don't do this wicked thing! What about me! Where could I get rid of my disgrace?" (2 Sam. 12:12–13 NIV).

Tamar wasn't just looking out for herself—she was as genuinely concerned about Amnon. "What about you? You'd be like one of the wicked fools in Israel. Please speak to the King; he will not keep me from being married to you" (2 Sam. 12:13 NIV).

Amnon's lust, however, erupted; he would not listen and he raped her. The Word carefully assigns the responsibility to Amnon "since he was stronger than she" (2 Sam. 13:14 NIV) and apparently because the writer did not want to blemish Tamar's good name.

After the assault, Amnon's mood changed immediately. "Get up and get out!" (2 Sam. 13:15 NIV). She tried to reason with him but he stubbornly refused to listen. Then, to add insult to injury, he ordered his servant: "Get this woman out of here and bolt the door after her" (2 Sam. 13:15 NIV).

After raping Tamar's body, he raped her *reputation* by nourishing the servant's impression that Tamar had seduced Amnon—the ultimate insult!

Imagine what that moment must have been like for her. She must have been stately and proud, elegantly dressed in special robes as a daughter of the king—but Amnon had treated her worse than a slave. She broke into tears and ripped her gown.

We would expect someone to help Tamar. Yet, when her brother Absalom discovered the situation, he suggested keeping it in the family. Actually he said: "Don't take this thing to heart" (2 Sam. 13:20 NIV) —as if he were talking about an offense like namecalling, rather than rape.

So this beautiful woman had to live with the crushing burden that she had been raped *by her own brother* and was powerless to do anything about it. Her future had been sacrificed upon the altar of his immediate sexual needs.

Tamar's unexpected *big event* forever altered the direction of her life.

Have you talked to anyone who has been raped? Once, after speaking in a college chapel on intimacy, I was approached by a student who wanted to talk to me. I suggested a time a couple of days later, but she insisted, "I need to talk to you *now!*"

When we met in private, she wasted no time in blurting out: "I've been raped." As she told her story, I was appalled at the judgmental attitude surfacing within me: *She probably asked for it.* I had thought that my ideas that women's dress was related to rape had been dissolved by Susan Brownmiller's *Against Our Will.* But the thoughts continued to tumble through my mind.

As I researched *A Part of Me Is Missing,* I discovered that most evangelical men do not really believe a woman's no means *no!* One guy responded, "She'd like to say yes, but if she said yes, I'd think badly of her." There are some women (and some men) who have found themselves in compromising situations and have "given in," saying yes to a level of intimacy to which they really wanted to say no. The guy did not think it was *rape.*

And many women hide the fact that they have been raped—because they fear what the police might do to them or what the defendant's attorney might drag up from their past. And forever after, they are labeled, too often not as an innocent victim of a crime, but as a participant in their own degradation and humiliation.

So it is easy—too easy—to label ourselves like Hester Prynne in *The Scarlet Letter* because of something that has happened to us. Some of us walk around years later with a big "R" stamped on us for *raped;* or a big "D" for *divorced;* or a big "W" for *widowed;* or a big "P" for *poor;* or a big "L" for *lonely;* or a big "U" for *unsuccessful;* or a big "F" for *failure.*

Constantly talking of the past, sifting through the debris looking for new clues—trying to find pieces that fit, trying to refight old battles, or right old wrongs is counterproductive and exhausting.

The burden periodically reminds us of its residency. So, week after week, year after year, sometimes decade after decade, we struggle under its oppressive weight.

Have you ever prayed for forgiveness, taking comfort in the confession?

I remember a friend whose "way with women" I envied. His idea of a double date was not the conventional one of sharing his car with another couple—but having two dates on the same night! Yet Monday morning chapel service found him on his knees, confessing his latest transgression. Time after time, he let the Lord relieve his guilt over the sin—but he did not want to open his life to what the Lord could do with his need. So the cycle of sin repeated itself—and he was unable to experience true repentance.

When we merely confess our sin without repenting, without that "turning away," little things seem to set off our mental videotapes of those sinful incidents we would prefer to forget.

"Oh, no!" you cry. "I don't want to think about it! Satan, get behind me!" It's easy to conclude that Satan, the enemy, is responsible for the videotape. So, on the fourth replay, you turn up the volume on your prayer. But *why* do we continue to see those unpleasant reminders of our failures?

Could it be that the Lord wants to reveal the *reasons* behind the sin, and, by exposing our spiritually vulnerable points, to deal with our *need* as well as with our *sin?*

The writer of Hebrews encouraged us to "throw off everything that hinders and the sin that so easily entangles" (Heb. 12:1 NIV)—that which trips us up.

Even those haunting sins seemingly beyond our control can be deleted from our list of concerns.

Tragically "Tamar lived in her brother Absalom's house, a desolate woman" (2 Sam. 13:20 NIV). But this side of the cross event, this side of the Resurrection, there are those contemporary Tamars who live devastated lives because of one unnecessary failure.

One of my graduate school projects involved directing a weekend retreat for college students and couples interested in ministry to them. The weekend failed to reach most of its outlined goals and was a financial disaster. The critique I wrote for the professor analyzed precisely what had caused these failures. Expecting no higher grade than a *B-,* I was amazed when I received an *A.* Upon my inquiry, the professor justified my grade, explaining that the purpose of any field project was to *learn.* My failures taught me how to plan better and to better implement my resources, ensuring more successful future retreats.

And I also learned from the faclure of my marriage. I had never dreamed *my* marriage would fail. But it did! After my divorce, I told the Lord, *If You really* (and *really* was emphasized in my prayer) *love me, You'll help me meet someone to take away all this pain.* I thought a second marriage would be the answer to my loneliness.

I'm glad the Lord didn't answer my selfish prayer. He taught me that He wants to heal us on *His* timetable with *His* methods. Many wounded people jump into a second marriage prematurely rather than building a foundation for healing and forgiveness or reconciliation.

David apparently neither confronted his son nor comforted his daughter—not exactly a fantastic example of fatherhood. Absalom plotted and planned against Amnon, fueling a family nightmare which finally erupted into flame with Absalom's murder of Amnon.

Revenge is always nasty business. Like permanent ink in the hands of a student learning to use a fountain pen, it always causes spills and stains. And resentment is a conscious decision to nourish the hurt—preserving the scab and postponing the scar.

The kid who finds a bear cub and thinks he can keep it in a cage discovers that eventually the cub becomes a full-grown bear, wreaking all kinds of havoc. More than one wild animal trainer has had his pet turn on him.

Similarly we think we can assign limits to the growth of our hatred or anger. As I observed in *Warm Reflections*, there are people who never pet a rattlesnake, or purposely wreck a car, or drink poison, but who keep attitudes and emotions as destructive as radioactive waste stored in their spirits.

We serve a God who can bring beauty from ashes.

Two weeks before I was scheduled to attend a banquet for Christian writers, a letter arrived from a major publisher to whom I had submitted a manuscript. They were interested! I thought they were going to offer me a contract; everything was looking good. . . . Boy, was I going to have something to brag about at that banquet!

Two days before the banquet, however, a large brown envelope landed with a distinctive thump on my desk. I didn't need to open it—I recognized the return address. My manuscript had been rejected!

Well, I had paid too much for the ticket to the banquet not to use it. I psyched myself up in front of the bathroom mirror to gain courage.

As I entered the hotel lobby, I ran into Dr. Sherwood Wirt, host of the banquet and former editor of *Decision*. "Well, how are things going?" he queried cheerfully.

"Awful! I just got turned down by _____ ." I expected him to join me in my lamentation.

"Big deal! Everyone gets turned down—even me!"

Licking my wounds, I crept off to find my seat, which turned out to be next to an attractive young woman. We engaged in the normal prebanquet "Wonder-what's-on-the-menu?" kind of conversation one has with someone he's never seen before and probably will never see again.

She asked, "Are you a writer?"

"Why, yes, I am," I responded, inwardly disappointed that she did not recognize my name. A blitzkrieg of what I had published took us through the salad and into the entree. Actually I unleashed a lot of my angry feelings, bemoaning my recent rejection slip.

The woman listened. "You know, this is fortunate for me to sit here next to you since you are a *writer* (the emphasis on the word *writer* was a boost to my ego) . . . because I really *want* to write."

I shuddered. Was I going to have to listen to another of those "God-and-me" stories that someone thinks ought to be in print?

Since we had only a few minutes before the program started, I thought it was safe to let her talk.

"I'm here tonight to get away for a while from some . . . problems.

"My husband and I have been trying to have a baby for ten years. While we were in med school we decided to wait. I went back to school and got my master's degree. When my husband finished school, we thought we could start a family *and* a practice.

"Finally, we decided to adopt."

Well, if anyone should be able to adopt, I thought, *this couple should—great income, beautiful home.*

"But even after all the paperwork and interviews, years went by without our finalizing an adoption. Then I got pregnant."

By this time, most of the guests at the table had ended their conversation to tune in to ours. "On April 1 (a few weeks earlier), Scott was born."

Now I understood what she had meant by "problems"—with a new baby in the house, this was probably her first venture out of the house. I opened my mouth to offer congratulations, but shut it again as she continued, "He died that night."

No one at the table was ready for that sentence. Dessert was ignored as she explained just how tough were those frustrating years of trying to have a baby and going through the red tape of the adoption process, finally getting pregnant, and losing the baby after one day!

Each of us searched the eyes of our fellow listeners, pleading, "Someone say *something.*" But what could be said in such a moment? This woman didn't need any more platitudes—she'd already had a platterful.

"So, what do you want to write. . . ?" I asked.

"I want to share with others the fact that in any experience, in any pain, in our crushing disappointments, Christ stands with us."

I felt chastised. She had desired only one label—"mother"—and that had been given her for just one day. Yet, here I was, griping over a book manuscript that had been rejected.

My new friend had walked through hell and stood to praise the Lord, without a hint of anger or resentment.

What has happened in your life over which you can't gain victory—that "returns" periodically to haunt you? Forgiveness—even of those unmentionable, unbelievable experiences—must be preceded by a decision, an act of courage.

Only through such a decision can we gain victory over the "I-can't-believe-it-happened-to-me" incidents of life.

III

Serving the
Apprenticeship

The Apprenticeship

In plumbing, baking, carpentry, electronics, and other trades, a period of apprenticeship under the watchful eye of a master is required—a custom as old as mankind. Most professions also demand a period of supervision for new colleagues before they are fully credentialed.

As a writer, I will be forever indebted to Sherwood Wirt, editor emeritus of *Decision* magazine. His "shop"—a Point Loma College creative writing class—helped sharpen my skills, along with a summer conference for aspiring writers at Forest Home Conference Center and the critique group of the San Diego Guild of Christian Writers. I have accepted his suggestions for improving a sentence or paragraph, applied them, and had the delight of discovering they work! I've learned to love him because as

147

an "old pro" who "knows the ropes" (he hates clichés), he has willingly invited apprentices into his world.

Forgiveness also requires an apprenticeship. During a difficult period of my life, I saw the movie *The Hiding Place*. The conclusion was inescapable: My problems were insignificant compared to those faced victoriously by Corrie Ten Boom three decades before. Corrie Ten Boom had mastered the art of forgiveness. I discovered I was still a novice.

Because I know nothing about plumbing or electricity, I pay a professional to pull up in my driveway in his "shop on wheels" and do the work for me. I can always count on him to do the work professionally and accurately.

Unfortunately I cannot hire anyone to do my forgiving for me. Certainly there are those times when I ask for advice, when I look through the "manuals" or "how-to" books on forgiveness. Ultimately, however, I must stand before the One who earned the distinction "Master" on a dark afternoon nearly 2000 years ago. His final acts were acts of forgiveness. He forgave a thief (his last neighbor). And in a magnificent appeal to His Father, He forgave His murderers. "Father, forgive them for they do not know what they are doing" (Luke 23:34 NIV).

In the trades, apprentices are constantly evaluated and appraised. The Master often steps into my workshop and moves unhurriedly among the projects, examining each one closely and offering suggestions. Occasionally, there are moments of quiet affirmation—the pride of the Teacher in the work of His student. Then a smile, a nod, a word.

On other occasions, there have been frowns or sighs when it is evident that I have not yet learned the technique. Again, He takes time to deal with me patiently. He does not say, "Would you listen, *this time?*"

As this book reaches the bookstores and book-racks and ultimately finds its way into your library, there is a sense of anxiety—for surely the Enemy will create a situation which will tempt me to contradict what I have written. "Better practice what you preach, Mr. Towner!" someone may say. Or "He needs to read his own book!"

I can only hope that in such a moment, my fellow apprentices will encourage me to resume my journey.

Please do not call me an expert. If you do, I will only disappoint you. There is only one Master who has perfected the art of forgiveness. He does not hide His workmanship away in dusty cases—but displays it proudly in the public marketplace.

Will you become His apprentice and join with the numbers of others who are sharpening their forgive-ness skills in their quest toward being more like the Master?

Forgiving and Forgetting

The moment Christ forgives you, there is a massive bonfire in the archives of eternity. The charred pieces of your sin record cannot be pieced back together again—not even in anything that resembles those sophisticated TV crime labs.

Satan can produce the evidence to prove you're spiritually guilty. But he can do so *only* on the large screen of your mind *and with your cooperation!* When God forgives He does not microfilm your sin for historic preservation, but destroys even the memory of the sin.

I think some of our prayers require data God has chosen to forget. We keep bringing up things He doesn't remember. At those times, maybe God says, "What is Towner talking about?"

I query, *Don't You remember?*

Without hesitation God responds, "No."

Sometimes we jar someone's memories or prime his memory pump. Gradually the light begins to dawn—"It sounds kinda familiar." When you give him a few more details, he smiles and says, "Oh, yeah, now I remember. I had forgotten about that."

And maybe to prove that he remembers, *he* starts providing a few details. "Yeah, that's right," you respond.

But God promises "to remember (our) sins no more"(Heb. 8:12 NIV). Little hints don't jog His memory. The biblical record is clear: When God forgives, He forgets. The psalmist asked, "If you, O Lord, kept a record of sins, O Lord, who could stand? But with you there is forgiveness; therefore you are feared" (Psalm 130:3–4 NIV). It seems ironic that we're fearful of those who know something about us while the Word insists that we should fear the One who gives complete forgiveness. This led Paul to write, "(Love) keeps no record of wrongs" (1 Cor. 13:5 NIV).

When I was a child in Sunday school, we used to sing a classic chorus:

> Gone, gone, gone, gone
> Yes, my sins are gone!

It was a good chorus, ranking number two in our top ten, and almost edging out, "Do Lord!" (obviously the "Hallelujah Chorus" of many evangelicals). "Gone! Gone! Gone! Gone!" was easily memorized and didn't have sharps or flats, which meant Henrietta Wilson could always play it.

Everyone in Ina Quiggins' Sunday school class learned the words and tune, even though it really isn't all that theologically profound or sound.

We always sang choruses twice: once, as a warm-up for the words and tune, and again, for proclamation. Often the teachers divided the class into sections to see who could sing (or scream) loudest.

So, here's the song—just in case you missed it. If you know the words, sing along:

> Gone! Gone! Gone! Gone!
> Yes, my sins are gone!
> Now my soul is free
>   and in my heart's a song.
> Buried in the deepest sea
> Yes, that's good enough for me.
> I shall live eternally
> Praise God!
> My sins are gone:
> g-o-n-e, gone!

Well, there is a lot of theological truth in that classic. My sins *are* gone and will not be remembered against me, ever again, under any circumstances—at least, by God. Unfortunately my enemies will use anything they can get their hands on.

We always emphasized the phrase, "Buried in the deepest sea." And another line suggested "In the sea of God's forgetfulness, yes, that's good enough for me!"

But just how deep is "the sea of God's forgetfulness"? According to *National Geographic,* the seas and oceans have places that are

    10,000 feet deep
    20,000 feet deep
    30,000 feet deep—

deep deep; no-way-to-touch-bottom deep. Depths so great that they can only be estimated.

So I relax and say, "Praise the Lord!"

But along comes the oceanographer, Jacques Cousteau, with a fleet of special submarines and equipment which *can* explore and photograph the bottom of the oceans and seas. On more than one occasion, following a sermon on forgiveness, I have sought confirmation of the depth of the seas from those pictures.

Some may think that all that photography was done at the bottom of Disneyland's "20,000 Leagues Under the Sea," but I have a hunch old Jacques has done his homework. He and/or his equipment have gone to the depths.

I learned "Gone! Gone! Gone! Gone!" before I knew about Cousteau's activities. Is my theology threatened by a photographer?

What if, as Jacques bumps around on the bottom of the ocean taking a million pictures of shipwrecks and weird-looking fish and flora, he finds a tombstone inscribed:

HERE LIE ALL THE MEAN, WICKED,
EVIL THINGS
JASON TOWNER HAS EVER SAID, DONE,
OR THOUGHT?

Catch on? Let's insert your name on the tombstone:

HERE LIE ALL THE MEAN, WICKED,
EVIL THINGS
_____ HAS EVER SAID, DONE,
OR THOUGHT.

You might want to scratch out some of those words on *your* tombstone and use milder synonyms.

What if someone starts digging in my past and finds out about. . . ? I sure hope "Gone! Gone! Gone! Gone!" is right, or I'm a *goner!*

I worry that if you knew about some incident in my past, you might close this book or even take it back for a refund. "I'm not reading another word written by such a man!"

I suspect my sins aren't really "buried" in the

deepest sea or in any sea. They're gone, vanished, exist no more. Oh, how desperately I want to believe that! But it is easier said than believed.

Something within us immediately responds, "Oh, yes, I hope that's true." We've all watched TV detective shows in which a private investigator searches and probes for the elusive evidence necessary to prove a client innocent.

Perhaps the evidence once existed but seemingly now has been destroyed. So it is with God. The evidence is gone; the record, erased.

Well, if God keeps no record, why do we? Paul insisted, "Forgive as the Lord forgave you" (Col. 3:13 NIV).

But what if they repeat the offense? Jesus said that we are to forgive "seventy times seven" (Matt. 18:22). If we imitate the Lord's forgiveness, we must *forget* as well as forgive. Thus, the statement: "I'll forgive you but I won't forget it" is blasphemy.

"For they shall all know me, from the *least* of them unto the greatest of them, saith the Lord: for I will forgive their iniquity, and *I will remember their sin no more*" (Jer. 31:34, *italics mine*).

Job, in defending himself from his "friends" who insisted that he had sinned, suggested: "I sinned . . . but I did not get what I deserved" (Job 33:27 NIV). Many contemporary Jobs could nod in agreement.

And the writer of Hebrews footnoted Jeremiah's words of comfort and assurance: "I will forgive their wickedness and will remember their sins no more" (Heb. 8:12 NIV).

But the Person of Jesus makes the difference between the Old and the New Testament readings: "Jesus has become the guarantee of a better covenant" (Heb. 7:22 NIV).

In the preface to his remarks on forgiveness, the

writer states boldly, "Therefore he is able to save *completely* those who come to God through him, because he always lives to intercede for them" (Heb. 7:25 NIV, *italics mine*). I have marked that passage in yellow, underlined it, and placed two red stars in the column beside it. He saves me *completely* by forgetting.

A few chapters later, the writer returns to this theme, "Their sins and lawless acts I will remember no more" (Heb. 10:17 NIV).

Can it be that God really forgets?

"As far as the east is from the west, so far has he removed our transgressions from us" (Ps. 103:12 NIV).

Would you be willing to read and meditate on the promises of Psalm 103 and Psalm 51 every day for the next thirty days?

And, to help you hide their promises in your heart, would you be willing to type those Scriptures on a file card and place it on your bathroom mirror or on the refrigerator door or on the window over the kitchen sink?

David insisted, "I have hidden your word in my heart, that I might not sin against you" (Ps. 118: 11 NIV). We sin by discrediting Psalm 103, by putting in disclaimers that qualify or limit. His Word has no footnotes or asterisks. If it applies to anyone, it applies to you!

And we have one advantage over the psalmist: "If anybody does sin, we have one who speaks to the Father *in our defense*—Jesus Christ, the Righteous One" (1 John 2:1 NIV, *italics mine*). Thus the One who should be most offended by our sin, defends us.

Do you need to stop here for a while and use the moment to read Psalm 103, trusting the powerful assurance of His Word?

The majesty of forgiveness lies in its availability and Jesus is its guarantee!

However, our confidence is stolen by the few who refuse to believe this promise. Those who not only believe in backsliding but enthusiastically practice it have an additional problem.

God doesn't trot out the past to browbeat us, to indict us for the present, to humble us, to help us be more "spiritual." God doesn't remember our sins. While we generally praise a good memory as a virtue, a bad memory is God's greatest attribute!

What could happen in your home . . .

What could happen in your office . . .

What could happen in your bedroom . . .

What could happen in your church . . . if we had a moratorium on bringing up the past? I have a friend who was charged with conduct unbecoming a clergyman. For a while, this rather serious charge was fed by rumors. Finally I asked one woman who was convinced her pastor was guilty, "How can you be so sure?"

"How?" she demanded, outraged. "Because he was guilty of that very thing thirteen years ago!" The axiom, "once guilty, always guilty" claimed another victim.

So we live in constant fear that someone will discover something about our past or remember something at an awkward moment.

We fret over partially-forgiven sin and offense.

Though computers can store a great number of facts and file cabinets can hold many reams of paper, they have capacity limits. Someone has to occasionally discard the old to make room for the new.

God doesn't forgive us to make room for new sins. God doesn't go through old scrapbooks one last time before destroying the evidence.

In a split second, a unit of time imperceptible to humanity, He *forgets*. In the language of eternity, there is but one word: *forgiven*. And its synonym is *forgotten*.

I wonder if adults can really understand the meaning of those words
> while sitting in stalled traffic,
> lying awake in the night hours,
> soaking in a tub,
> listening to the evening news.

Forgotten! Gone! How can I be certain?
So they ask, "How do I forget, Jason Towner? How do *you* forget?"

I'm not always able to give an acceptable answer. Frankly, I'm still learning. But I do know what we say when we're tired:

"Forget it. It was nothing." (Although some people insist on inserting exclamation marks!)

"I'm tired of hearing about it. Just forget it!"

"How *could* you forget a thing like that?"

"I'll never forget the time . . ."

How do *you* forget, my friend whose name I do not know? Maybe you have the answer we're all looking for.

Forgetting is part of the process of forgiving. God leads the way and we must follow. If we will forget and make a decision to keep forgetting (that is, not periodically reviewing our hurts), we are well on the way to forgiving.

God suspends the laws of the universe only to forgive and forget your sin. The ultimate act of love, the ultimate beauty, is when God forgets.

But we, perhaps because of our scientific sophistication, want to use psychological jargon or processes; we want five easy steps to forgiveness.

Simply, He forgives.

When I give up trying to understand the process and concentrate on enjoying the promises, I can believe I am forgiven.

Wouldn't it be great if all the evangelical churches

in America took one day's offerings and carved the words "You are forgiven!" on Mt. Rushmore? Or pasted them on a series of gigantic billboards in heavy traffic areas? Paul said it so clearly, "There is now no condemnation for those who are in Christ Jesus" (Rom. 8:1 NIV). If only the people of God could remember that there are no strings attached to that promise! Nowhere is there the suggestion: "Well, except for the following . . ."

In 1979, I presented much of the material that now makes up this book. In one session I noticed a man visibly moved by the material, but because of the crowd, I wasn't able to get over to talk with him.

Late that night, as I was on my way to dinner with my editor, a woman stopped me.

"Are you Jason Towner?" she asked.

"Yes, I am."

"I want to talk to you. My husband came back to the room a changed man after your seminar."

I must have looked surprised, because she continued: "My husband has been involved in a situation and, though it is past, and I have forgiven him, he can't get over it. There are times he really gets depressed and the guilt is dragged out.

"Today we decided to go to different seminars and then agreed to meet back at the room for lunch. When he came through the door, I knew something had happened. For the first time in years, he knows he's been forgiven."

It was somewhat difficult for me to keep my composure. God used me to help another pilgrim find the fountain of forgiveness, and he had splashed in its healing waters as enthusiastically as any child in an inflatable swimming pool in the back yard on a hot August day.

Forgiveness is a reality and a decision. God has done His part. Now, will you accept His gift? That, too, is a decision.

Today, I can sing the last line of the chorus with an enthusiasm I never knew when I sang in junior church. "Praise God ... my sins are gone!" and naturally I add an exclamation mark.

So can you.

Finally

We've come to the end of *Forgiveness Is For Giving*. We've lost a few pilgrims en route; some people don't want to forgive.

I hope you're not the same person as when you began reading this book, because I'm not the same person as when I began writing it. I am more aware of the blessings of forgiveness; yet, am equally aware that I need to be more forgiving. This book was written by a fellow pilgrim, not an expert.

People say, "I'd like to do what you do." Or, "I think I could write a book." Or, "All that traveling sounds like a lot of fun . . ."

They see the glamour—but they don't see the Sunday nights I fly "home" to Kansas City (hoping my luggage will make it) and head toward Eighty-first Street in a VW with 100,000 miles on it.

Suddenly I'm not "the speaker" anymore. Although I've autographed books, answered questions, listened to problems, and shared with groups, now I am just another homeowner on Eighty-first Street. Most people don't care where I've been. They want to know when a project is going to be done or, sometimes, why it wasn't finished before I left on Friday.

I cannot forget the lady who arrogantly demanded, "Are you in this for God or for the money?"

I laughed. "Lady, anyone who knows anything about Christian writing knows that, for most of us, there's little money in it." I'm still thirty days away from the poorhouse, driving my VW, and eating at McDonald's at least twice a week.

So, why do I do it?

Because of guys like Bill, a Navy pilot. When his wife left him, Bill crawled under a blanket and stuffed a towel into his mouth so no one could see or hear him crying—such behavior could threaten his promotion. Now he's reading books and attending programs and seminars, looking for answers.

Or Mel, who came to all the sessions but sat against the wall in the foyer. He's hurting—but afraid to let go, to trust anyone. He's a desperate martyr.

Or Susan, who took careful notes and will no doubt reread the Scripture passages I used. She'll try forgiveness, but by Tuesday will doubt its reality. She wants a destination rather than a journey; she wants easily memorized black-and-white answers.

I see in many people the memories of my season of hurt. *My yesterdays*—the days when I cried alone and was ashamed of my tears—are *their todays*. But, we don't escape—we're all pilgrims even those behind the layers of cosmetic disguise.

I remember a 275-pound man who looked for answers, who blubbered, who was angry and hurt—a loser. Now people pay that same man to come to their groups and churches or conferences as a 190-pound speaker and author. Something within me says: *O God, help me to reach out to the heavy guy on the sixth row, and that lady over there. Help me to breathe Your Word on the cold embers to spark them to life.*

People—they're what keep me traveling and writing. People whose lives may be touched.

And this book has been written in an effort to help all those Bills, and Mels, and Susans—and "me's" and "you's"—along our forgiveness pilgrimage.

Only by sharing the principles and the promises of forgiveness can we be a part of its growth.

If forgiveness is stored, it loses its potency. Forgiveness is not a passive process, but an active, demanding journey. Too many people catalog all the hurts, disappointments, the "it-shouldn't-have-happened's" and place them in storage, in anticipation of some great religious service or revival or retreat. "Then I'll deal with them," they say.

But forgiveness has to happen in the *now.* Delay compounds or clouds the issue. Some problems mushroom with procrastination. An old song comes to mind:

> Got any rivers—you think are uncrossable
> Got any mountains you can't tunnel through
> God specializes in things thought impossible
> And He can do what no other power can do!

Forgiveness is always a decision. Forgiveness is as natural as the softness of a baby's skin.
It's unforgiveness that is learned behavior.
Unforgiveness is suicidal (and still is a decision).
Forgiveness is a journey—not a destination.
Most of us start on that journey with too much luggage. We need to discard some things on the side of the road.

The harshness of an editorial in the *Kansas City Star*, which suggested that forgiveness for Nazis "is out of the question" stunned me. The editorial did not appear in 1945 but on June 18, 1979.

I'm not condoning the Nazi war criminals and am concerned by the growth of the neo-Nazi movement today. But I would like to interview the doctor who was found guilty of murdering scores of inmates at the Mauthausen concentration camp while assigned there as a physician, 1941-1942. Court records reveal that he performed mock operations on the inmates and injected gasoline into their hearts. German authorities did not close in on him until 1962. But before they could arrest him, he fled. He has lived as a fugitive since, pursued by a professional Nazi-hunter. About what must he think and dream?

I would like to ask the hunter (who apparently will not rest as long as one Nazi criminal is unaccounted for) what *he* thinks and dreams about? What motivates him? Neither the hunter nor the hunted can rest. Both suffer under their burden.

I can't ask them, but I can ask you: "What is it like to be under *your* burden—twenty-four hours a day, seven days a week, 365 days a year?"

There is no statute of limitations with God nor is there double jeopardy. No forgiven sin will intolerably strain the conscience of God.

Forgiveness is for giving—and receiving. God wants you to enjoy His promise.

Christ has called us to participate in the work of forgiveness and of reconciliation (see 2 Cor. 5:19). He calls us as clearly as He did the day He said, "Forgive . . . so that your Father in heaven may forgive your sins" (Mark 11:25 NIV).

Forgiveness is for giving—and receiving. God invites you to enjoy His promise.

He could have kept this ministry to Himself—but His plan includes us. The Lord realized that some of us could accept forgiveness in our moment of need only if we had prepared for that forgiveness through forgiving others.

So He has included us in the fellowship of the forgiven. He has also provided filters of forgiveness: time, other people, His Spirit. Only someone who would profit by keeping you in bondage would accuse you of cowardice in not accepting His invitation.

Forgiveness is a decision.

Today could be a good day to make your decision.

DATE